Mexico

Mexico

Revised Edition

BY R. CONRAD STEIN

Enchantment of the World
Second Series

Children's Press®

A Division of Scholastic Inc.

NEW YORK   TORONTO   LONDON   AUCKLAND   SYDNEY
MEXICO CITY   NEW DELHI   HONG KONG
DANBURY, CONNECTICUT

Frontispiece: A girl at the Guelaguetza festival in Oaxaca

Consultant: Richard Grossman, Department of History, Northeastern Illinois University

Please note: All statistics are as up-to-date as possible at the time of publication.

Book production by Herman Adler Design

Library of Congress Cataloging-in-Publication Data

Stein, R. Conrad.
  Mexico, revised edition / by R. Conrad Stein—Rev. ed.
      p. cm. — (Enchantment of the World. Second series)
  Includes index.
  ISBN-10: 0-516-24868-5
  ISBN-13: 978-0-516-24868-4
  1. Mexico—Juvenile literature. I. Title. II. Series.
  F1208.5.S73 2006
  972—dc22   2005024556

CHILDREN'S PRESS and associated logos are trademarks and/or registered
trademarks of Scholastic Library Publishing. SCHOLASTIC and associated logos
are trademarks and/or registered trademarks of Scholastic Inc.
1 2 3 4 5 6 7 8 9 10 R 16 15 14 13 12 11 10 09 08 07

Mexico

Cover photo:
A Mexican girl carries decorations for Day of the Dead celebrations.

Contents

Mexican village

Olmec sculpture

Three Cultures, Three Identities

IN THE HEART OF BUSY MEXICO CITY SPREADS A BROAD PUBLIC square called the Plaza of Three Cultures. Here, buildings from the three great chapters of Mexican history stand almost side by side. In one corner of the plaza are the ruins of a pyramid constructed many hundreds of years ago by the Aztec. Nearby rises a gray stone church built by the Spaniards in the 1600s. Towering over both structures is a modern glass and steel apartment building. Nowhere in Mexico do the three stories of a nation—its indigenous past, its Spanish colonial past, and its modern period—come together so neatly as they do in this plaza. The Mexican people have also been shaped by the country's threefold past. The vast majority of Mexicans are a mixture of European and indigenous blood.

The past is imprinted on Mexico's cities and villages. Most older towns

Opposite: **Almost all Mexicans have both indigenous and European ancestors.**

The Church of Santiago was built in 1609. It sits in the Plaza of Three Cultures on top of an Aztec pyramid built hundreds of years earlier.

have at their heart a tree-shaded plaza where villagers sit on benches and read the morning newspapers. Modern Mexico begins several blocks away from the old plaza. There factories sprawl over what was once farmland. Clustered around the factories are the modest houses where workers live. Traffic jams are now the rule in modern neighborhoods.

People relax in the shade of the plaza in Bernal.

Mexico is like the flower beds that most Mexican house-holds keep and adore. Just as the flowers burst with different colors, Mexico is alive with contrasts. The land embraces towering mountains, vast deserts, and lovely ocean beaches. In the cities, fabulously wealthy houses rise next to the shacks of the poor.

Some Mexican houses are covered in plants. The green brings a cool, refreshing feeling to the often hot country.

As is true with many other industrializing nations, the Mexican economy fails to provide for all its people. Hardworking men and women have to struggle to keep their jobs and pay bills. But just to the north lies *El Norte*, as the Mexicans call the United States, which has the richest economy on earth. Nowhere else in the world does a developing nation lie so close to a wealthy nation. The lure is great for young Mexicans to migrate north—either legally or illegally—and prosper in that richer land.

Despite its economic problems, Mexico is a vibrant country. It is a place where music and laughter ring out on the streets. Outsiders are often stunned by the friendliness Mexicans show to those from other countries. It is as if a welcome sign hangs above every house. Mexico is a land full of richness and surprises.

Music and festivals are a central part of life in Mexico. Here, a dancer performs in Acapulco.

An Exciting Land

IN THE YEAR 1521, A SPANISH ARMY LED BY HERNANDO Cortés completed the conquest of the mighty Aztec nation of central Mexico. After his victory, Cortés returned to Spain, where the king asked him to describe this new land in the Americas. Cortés stammered, pointed upward, and drew wide circles with his finger. The king shifted impatiently on his throne. Finally, according to legend, Cortés grabbed a piece of paper, crumpled it into a ball, and presented it to his king. He said, "There, your Majesty, Mexico looks like this."

Never before had Cortés seen such a place where jagged mountain peaks rise above the clouds and seem to kiss the sky. The Spanish conqueror had described the rugged Mexican landscape the best way he could.

Opposite: **The beach at Acapulco is lined with hotels. Millions of people visit the city every year.**

Rugged mountains slice through Mexico. The peaks of the Sierra Madre Occidental rise to between 5,000 feet (1,500 m) and 10,000 feet (3,000 m).

An Exciting Land **15**

A glance at a map shows that Mexico is a long, narrow country that grows even narrower in the south. A drive along its west coast, from the U.S. border in the north to Guatemala in the south, takes almost as long as driving across the width of United States. In area, Mexico covers 756,066 square miles (1,958,201 square kilometers). This makes Mexico the fifth-largest country in the Americas, after Canada, the United States, Brazil, and Argentina.

Two gigantic mountain ranges—the Sierra Madre Oriental (*oriental* means "east") and the Sierra Madre Occidental (*occidental* means "west")—run the length of Mexico. A central

The mountains meet the sea near Calvario Beach on the Pacific Ocean.

plateau, called the Plateau of Mexico, lies between the two ranges. Normally, a plateau is an elevated, flat expanse of land. But few places are flat in Mexico. The Plateau of Mexico has steep hills, towering mountains, and cone-shaped volcanoes. This vast Plateau of Mexico is the nation's heartland. It contains Mexico's richest farmland and largest cities. Throughout its history, most of the nation's people have lived on the Plateau of Mexico.

At 18,410 feet (5,610 m), Citlaltépetl is the highest peak in Mexico. It is the third-highest in North America.

The Yucatán Peninsula is famous for both its beautiful beaches and its ancient Mayan sites. At Tulúm, the ruins of a Mayan temple lie right next to the sea.

Mexico's two mountain ranges taper down to the seacoasts. The Pacific coast, and more than 2,000 miles (3,200 km) of seashore, lie to the west. The Caribbean Sea and the Gulf of Mexico spread to the east. This wealth of coastline includes the sunny beaches that give Mexico its reputation as a vacationer's paradise.

In the south, the Yucatán Peninsula juts out to the east. As in much of southern Mexico, rain forests and grassy plains stretch across the land.

Geographical Features

Area: 756,066 square miles (1,958,201 sq km)

Highest Elevation: Citlaltépetl (also called Orizaba), 18,410 feet (5,610 m)

Lowest Elevation: Mexicali Valley, 33 feet (10 m) below sea level

Longest River: Lerma River, 350 miles (563 km)

Largest City: Mexico City

Average Annual Precipitation: Mexico City, 30 inches (76 cm); Monterrey, 23 inches (58 cm)

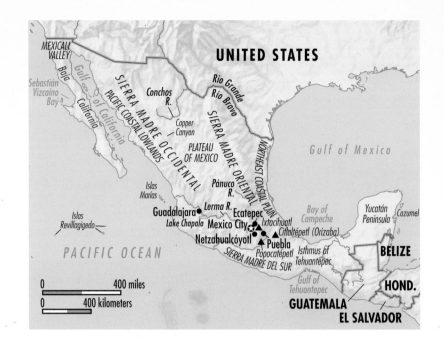

A Gentle Climate

People from Canada and the northern United States are astonished when they first visit Mexico. Business is conducted in the open air because most stores have no front wall. Instead, they have overhead doors like those on garages. At night, the storekeeper simply pulls the door down and locks it. Street vendors spread their goods on sidewalks, hoping to lure customers. Because of the warm climate, this outdoor business continues even in the middle of January.

Mexico's gentle climate encourages outdoor living. Even during winter months, people on the Plateau of Mexico wear light clothing, though they may have to wear a jacket at night. Summers are pleasant, too. The Plateau of Mexico averages about 6,000 feet (1,800 meters) above sea level. Because of this high altitude, it is rarely humid, making air-conditioning unnecessary.

In Mexico, temperatures are not necessarily warmer in the southern part of the country. Instead, temperature changes with elevation. The heat and humidity increase as one descends from the Plateau of Mexico to the seacoast. The area at sea level is called the *tierra caliente*, the "hot land." People in the hot land must learn to live with the sticky heat.

Mexicans enjoy another warm day at the beach.

A Look at Mexico's Cities

"Guadalajara! Guadalajara! You are the soul of the province; you have the lovely smell of an early rose," says a lively song praising Mexico's second-largest city. Like all the nation's cities, Guadalajara (above) has suffered in recent years from overpopulation and air pollution. Still it delights visitors with its fountains, public squares, and tree-shaded parks. The city's restaurants are said to be the best in Mexico. A frothy stew called *pozole* is a favorite Guadalajaran dish.

Puebla (right), Mexico's fourth-largest city, has a strong Spanish influence. A thousand buildings from the Spanish colonial era grace central Puebla. Many are decorated with the hand-painted tiles for which the city is famous. The city is also famous for a spicy sauce called *mole poblano*, which has a hint of chocolate to it. Mole poblano is served over chicken or other foods.

World-Famous Beach Resorts

Sun worshippers and water lovers from around the world flock to the hot lands for vacations. They crowd the endless silvery beaches. The city of Acapulco on the Pacific coast has drawn foreign visitors since the 1940s. The most popular tourist spot in recent years is Cancún, on the Gulf of Mexico.

Mexico's gentle climate has one persistent problem: a lack of rain. In the Plateau of Mexico, home to the country's best farmland, the rainy season starts in May and lasts until October. If rain does not fall during those months, the farmers despair. Sometimes the entire population of a farming village will go to the fields and pray for the rains to begin. Some farm families hold the statue of a saint up to the heavens and beg the saint to send rain. Older farmers might silently pray to Tláloc, the ancient Aztec rain god.

Tláloc, the Rain God

More than five hundred years ago, the Aztecs regarded Tláloc as the giver or withholder of rain. Thus Tláloc was a powerful god in this often parched land. The Aztecs dutifully carved stone statues of Tláloc and worshipped the figures. In 1964, workers removed a centuries-old 60-ton (54-metric-ton) statue of Tláloc from a rural village and set it up at the entrance of the new Museum of Anthropology in Mexico City. Villagers had warned that the move would make Tláloc angry. Just days after the statue was put in place, Mexico City was struck with a devastating rainstorm. It was the worst off-season storm in memory and caused severe flooding.

Risky Grounds

September 19, 1985, began like any other day in Mexico City. The sun rose. The morning traffic jam began. Then, just after 7:00 A.M., high-rise buildings suddenly swayed like palm trees bending in the wind. Windows shattered, and glass rained down on the sidewalks.

At once, Mexico City residents understood. "*Terremoto!*" shouted people on the sidewalks. "Earthquake!"

Floors in downtown buildings collapsed on top of each other. A man on the twelfth floor of an apartment building said he felt a hollow sensation in his stomach, as if he were in an elevator plunging downward. Buildings that were ten stories high compacted to four stories in a matter of minutes. Thousands of people were buried under tons of debris.

The 1985 earthquake lasted only a few seconds, but it was the worst natural disaster to strike Mexico in modern times. So violent was the tremor that it shook buildings 600 miles (1,000 km) away in Texas. The government later announced that up to ten thousand people had died, but many experts claim the number of deaths was twice that high. At least one hundred thousand people were left homeless.

The people of Mexico City cleaned up their streets and buried their dead after the 1985 earthquake. They went on with their lives, trying not to wonder when the next disaster

The 1985 earthquake completely destroyed 412 buildings in Mexico City. Another 3,100 were severely damaged.

Land of Volcanoes

Mexico has about three thousand volcanoes. Some, like Popocatépetl (left) near Mexico City, are active and sometimes spew gas and ash. New volcanoes can appear at any time. One volcano burst out of the ground 250 miles (400 km) southwest of Mexico City in 1943. It grew so rapidly that hundreds of farm families living nearby had to flee for their lives. In just two months, the volcano had become a cone-shaped mountain standing 1,000 feet (300 m) over what had been a cornfield.

would visit their city. But all Mexicans know that much of their country rests on unstable ground. Mexico is even more earthquake-prone than California. A particularly hazardous region lies to the south of Mexico City.

Despite drought, volcanoes, and earthquakes, Mexico is an uncommonly beautiful land. Anyone who has been there longs to go back and experience again the thrilling vistas of its mountains and seacoasts.

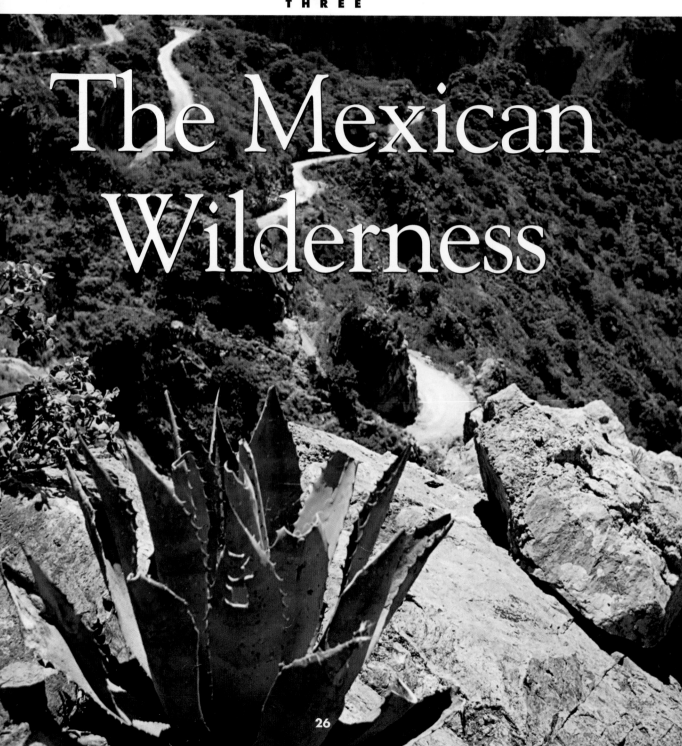

The Mexican Wilderness

Not that long ago, Mexico was alive with wild animals. Jaguars stalked the jungles of the Yucatán, while exotic birds skimmed the treetops. Deer grazed on the central plateau, and mountain lions roamed the Sierra Madre. These animals are still found in the Mexican wilds, but in vastly reduced numbers. Highways now connect just about every corner of the nation. The road system brings in hunters who shoot the game animals and farmers who plant crops on land where wildlife once ranged freely.

Opposite: **An agave plant clings to a rocky outcrop in the Copper Canyon.**

A highway cuts across the Plateau of Mexico. More than 200,000 miles (320,000 km) of road crisscross Mexico.

Yet Mexico's western Sierra Madre contains one sprawling land region that is simply too remote and too rugged for highway construction. South of the city of Chihuahua lies the Copper Canyon, a breathtaking gorge with four times the area of the Grand Canyon.

Time stands still in the canyon. Deer, bears, and mountain lions roam along the streams and in the patches of pine forests. The canyon is also home to about sixty thousand Tarahumara, an indigenous people who live mainly by farming and hunting. The Copper Canyon is a spectacular reminder of Mexico's wilderness in a bygone age.

The Copper Canyon is covered with forests of ponderosa pine and oak.

The Maya and the Jaguar

The Maya, who once lived in southern Mexico and the Yucatán region, developed an advanced civilization. Their astronomers plotted the passage of stars and planets with astonishing precision. The Maya worshipped the jaguar, a creature of the Yucatán rain forests. The jaguar god was thought to control the underworld, where people went after death. During religious festivals, Mayan priests wore colorful jaguar masks and chanted special prayers.

Mountain Life

The plants and animals of Mexico's mountains differ sharply from those found on the seacoasts. The mountain environment has nurtured a fantastic variety of plant and animal life.

A turkey vulture sits atop a cardon cactus. Turkey vultures prefer to live in open, unforested areas.

A hiker might get lucky and see a few of Mexico's large wild animals such as deer, bears, bobcats, and coyotes. But wildlife seekers in the mountains should keep their eyes on the sky and the ground. Vultures, some with 30-inch (76-centimeter) wingspans, fly above. They wheel around in graceful circles searching for dead animals to feast on. Snakes, rodents, and scurrying lizards are found at the hiker's feet. The rocky landscape of the mountains is alive with wild creatures.

Cardon cactuses thrive in dry regions like Baja California. Their large root systems quickly suck up water during the rare downpours, and their strong trunks can hold up to a ton of water.

The Plateau of Mexico has few trees, but it is home to a huge assortment of cactus plants. Cacti store water in their stems, allowing them to live in an almost rainless climate. Nearly a thousand different kinds of cacti grow in Mexico, many in the mountainous regions. The saguaro, or giant cactus, grows so tall that it looks like a tree. Some saguaros reach a height of 50 feet (15 m). The prickly pear cactus, which rises only knee-high to the average person, is a great help to farmers. They use the sharp-quilled cactus like barbed wire, planting rows of it to create pens for their cattle.

Mexicans eat some cactus plants. A flat-leaved cactus called nopal is stripped of its quills, cut into tiny pieces, and fried in oil. Fried nopal with scrambled eggs is often served for breakfast. A refreshing cactus fruit called tuna tastes something like watermelon. The reddish tuna is covered with a fine coat of needlelike quills that can be peeled away only by experienced hands.

Flat cactus pads called nopales are a common food in Mexico. Some people say they taste like green beans.

The Joy of Chiclets

Sit in a city park for more than ten minutes and you are sure to be approached by a child saying, "Chiclets, chiclets! Want to buy chiclets?" The child will then hold up a package of chewing gum. The gum is the famous chicle, which has been enjoyed in Mexico for ages. Chiclets are sometimes used as money. A shopkeeper who has no change will give you packages of chiclets in place of coins. Chiclets are made from the pulp of the sapodilla tree, which grows in wet areas of southern Mexico.

Life in the Lowlands

Mexico is a land of contrasts. The great plateau hosts sprawling deserts, while the lowlands to the south and west are swampy. Fruits such as mango and papaya grow in the wetlands. These fruits, along with bananas, oranges, and grapefruits, crowd stalls in southern markets. After heavy rains, the southern wetlands are ablaze with flowers—orchids, dahlias, and bougainvillea. Groves of coconut palms stand along the beaches.

Papayas grow only in areas that are warm year-round, such as the Yucatán Peninsula. Even brief freezing temperatures will kill them.

Flamingos use their long legs to wade into deep water to feed. They stick their bills underwater, suck up mud and water, and strain out the food.

Take a walk in the wetlands and you will hear a haunting chorus of birdcalls. Herons, ducks, and geese fly in the lagoons. Flocks of pink flamingos feed in the swamps of the Yucatán. The south has the country's richest variety of animal life.

An iguana's tail makes up about half its body length. If the tail gets broken off, it can grow back.

The speckled ocelot, which looks like a large cat, still stalks the southern forests. Spider monkeys swing along trees in the forests. Some spider monkeys are kept as pets, as are some iguanas. The iguana is a large, green lizard with a comblike row of scales running down its back. Alligators and poisonous snakes are also found in the Mexican tropics. No one makes pets out of these creatures.

The Vanishing Burro

Almost five hundred years ago, Spaniards brought donkeys (called *burros* in Spanish) to Mexico. The sturdy burro, a relative of the horse, became a fixture on Mexican farms and in villages. For generations, artists painting pictures of Mexican rural life portrayed the burro carrying loads or pulling farm wagons. The burro became a symbol of Mexico. Late in the twentieth century, many Mexicans began to replace their burros with tractors. But farmers soon discovered their new machines could not go over rugged mountain trails that the burros climbed with ease. An alarming burro shortage suddenly struck Mexico. In 2004, an official from the state of Jalisco imported fifty donkeys from Kentucky. Said one Jalisco farmer, the burros, "are so useful and such hard workers [that] we need more of them."

Mexicans still use burros for trips over rough land. This one is ready for a trip down into the Copper Canyon.

A Dramatic Past

Humans have lived in what is now Mexico for more than ten thousand years. The earliest people were bands of hunters who killed giant mammoths on the central plateau. In about 7000 B.C., the hunters learned how to grow corn. The hunting societies of Mexico gradually became farming societies. Farming gave the people stability and allowed them to develop advanced civilizations.

In about 1250 B.C., a people called the Olmec built farming communities near the Gulf of Mexico. Their most lasting monuments are huge stone heads up to 10 feet (3 m) tall. These giant faces have a curiously African look. Some historians suggest there was contact between the Olmec and African people in ancient times.

Sometime near 200 B.C., a mysterious civilization built a great city about 35 miles (55 km) north of present-day Mexico City.

Opposite: **Metropolitan Cathedral in Guadalajara is Mexico's third-largest church. It took fifty years to build.**

The faces carved on the giant heads by the Olmec are thought to be portraits of Olmec rulers.

At its most successful point, the ancient city held as many as 200,000 people. It was dominated by two massive pyramids that today are called the Pyramid of the Sun and the Pyramid of the Moon. For unknown reasons, that great city was abandoned and destroyed around A.D. 600–700. Today, its ruins attract millions of visitors. More than five hundred years ago, the Aztec people also held these ruins in awe. The Aztecs named the ghost city Teotihuacán ("the place where gods are born").

The Maya created one of Mexico's greatest civilizations, which was at its peak from A.D. 200 to 800. The Maya built vast cities in southern Mexico and Central America, and made many advances in mathematics and astronomy. The calendar the Maya devised was more accurate than any other in use at the time. The ancient Mayan civilization eventually declined, although Mayan people still live in southern Mexico. Some still speak their old language and observe the religious practices handed down by their ancestors.

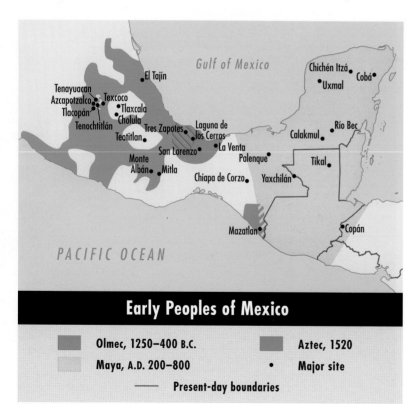

Early Peoples of Mexico

Olmec, 1250–400 B.C.   Aztec, 1520
Maya, A.D. 200–800   •   Major site
——— Present-day boundaries

The Aztec Empire

The greatest builders in ancient Mexico were the Aztecs. They had conquered other groups in Mexico to form a great empire. In about 1325, the Aztecs began constructing their masterpiece—the capital city of Tenochtitlán—on an island in the middle of a great, sparkling lake. The city had towering pyramids, ruler-straight streets, canals for boats carrying crops, and a marketplace where up to sixty thousand people bought and sold goods.

The Aztecs were a warrior people. Their gods demanded the ultimate gift—human sacrifice. Aztec soldiers led long lines of people to the tops of pyramids where priests cut out their hearts and held them, still beating, in front of a god's statue. They believed the hearts were needed to make the gods bless the nation with rain, good crops, and victory in war. Other ancient peoples in Mexico and Europe also practiced human sacrifice rituals, but few killed so many people in such brutal ways.

The Pyramid of the Sun rose 207 feet (63 m) high. Underneath it, a tunnel led to a group of rooms that were used for rituals.

Corn, a Gift from a God

The Aztecs and other ancient Mexicans told a story about how people got corn. Long ago, according to the legend, only the ants harvested and ate corn. The ants were determined to keep the corn for themselves. They would not share the nourishing food with humans. But one day, a god who loved humans turned himself into an ant and crawled into an anthill. Then the god carried out a kernel of corn and presented it to human beings.

Hernando Cortés met Montezuma in 1519. Two years later, the Spaniards would defeat the Aztecs.

One Aztec god, however, condemned human sacrifice. His name was Quetzalcóatl. This gentle deity preferred gifts of flowers and butterflies to bloody human hearts.

Spanish Rule

In 1519, an army of five hundred Spanish soldiers splashed ashore at the beach near the present-day city of Veracruz. Historians have summed up the Spaniards' mission in the Americas in three words: God, gold, and glory. The Spaniards were trying to convert the native peoples to their Roman Catholic faith, find gold, and achieve military conquest.

They were led by Hernando Cortés. As he marched inland, Cortés preached the Christian religion to the indigenous people he encountered. He also told them that human sacrifice was a sin. His actions alarmed Montezuma, the Aztec emperor. A war broke out between the Aztecs and the Spaniards. Many indigenous peoples, who had long hated the Aztecs because of the heavy taxes they imposed, fought side by side with the Spaniards. In 1521, the Spaniards and their allies conquered the Aztecs. The Spaniards established their own empire and called it New Spain.

The great city of Tenochtitlán did not survive the war. It was reduced to rubble during the fighting. The Spaniards immediately began building a new city over the wreckage of

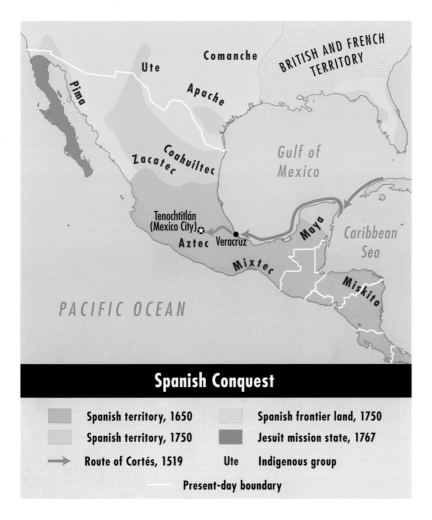

Spanish Conquest

■ Spanish territory, 1650	■ Spanish frontier land, 1750
■ Spanish territory, 1750	■ Jesuit mission state, 1767
→ Route of Cortés, 1519	Ute Indigenous group
— Present-day boundary	

Spanish Strength

Spanish soldiers brought guns, horses, and iron swords to the battlefield. Never before had the Aztecs fought against such well-armed men. The Spaniards also had a hidden weapon. Unknowingly, the soldiers carried European diseases to the Americas. The Europeans had lived with diseases such as smallpox and measles for hundreds of years. Their bodies had learned how to fight off these diseases, and people no longer died from them in large numbers. But indigenous Mexicans had never been exposed to these diseases before, so their bodies could not fight them off. In their final battles with the Spaniards, the Aztecs were so weakened by smallpox that many could hardly walk, much less fight. By 1581, the number of indigenous people in Mexico had dropped from an estimated fifteen million to fewer than two million.

the old. They used bricks from Aztec pyramids to construct houses and churches. The new city—Mexico City—served as the capital of New Spain for the next three hundred years.

Ghosts of Tenochtitlán

The ruins of old Tenochtitlán lie like coffins in a graveyard beneath the streets of Mexico City. Every now and then, those ancient coffins resurface. In the 1970s, construction workers came upon a vast temple complex buried below downtown Mexico City. The complex was carefully excavated, and it is now preserved as an outdoor museum called Templo Mayor (Main Temple).

After the conquest, thousands of Spaniards—mostly men—moved to New Spain, bringing with them the Spanish language and the Christian religion. The native Mexicans had no choice but to convert to Christianity. To them, the Catholic practice of praying to various saints was similar to their own religion in which they worshipped many gods.

A mysterious event that took place on the site of an old Aztec temple convinced many native Mexicans to adopt Catholicism. Both Spaniards and indigenous Mexicans hailed this event as a miracle. In January 1531, an indigenous man named Juan Diego climbed a hill near Mexico City. Juan Diego had recently become a Catholic. At the top of the hill, he saw a radiantly beautiful dark-skinned woman. She appeared to have a halo above her head. The woman said she wanted a church built on the spot where she stood. Juan Diego raced back to the city to tell the Spanish bishop what he had seen. The bishop asked Juan to bring some proof of his vision. Juan returned to the hilltop, and this time the woman gave him a bouquet of lovely roses. Juan tucked the roses into his straw coat and returned to show the flowers to the bishop. In the bishop's office, Juan opened his coat and the roses fell to the floor. The bishop was astonished, because painted on the inside of the jacket was a picture of the woman Juan had seen on the hilltop.

Nearly all Mexicans grow up hearing the tale of Juan Diego, his vision, and the miraculous picture on the straw jacket. The woman he saw is now called the Virgin of Guadalupe, and she is the patron saint of Mexico. Juan Diego's jacket hangs in a

Images of the Virgin of Guadalupe are everywhere in Mexico. She is adored both as a religious figure and as a symbol of Mexican pride.

frame at the church that was built where she is said to have appeared. Statues and paintings of her are all over Mexico. Poor families often have a figure made of straw, while wealthy people will proudly display a portrait of her in their living rooms. Rich or poor, Mexicans call her "our saint."

Since few Spanish women had moved to New Spain, Spanish men there had children with the Aztecs and other indigenous peoples. As a result, three classes of people emerged in Mexican society: whites, indigenous peoples, and a new group called the mestizos. The mestizos are people of mixed European and indigenous ancestry. After the Spanish conquest, the whites held all the power in New Spain. They allowed the mestizos some privileges but treated the indigenous people as a defeated people.

More than twelve thousand churches were built during the era of New Spain. Handsome cities such as Guadalajara, Guanajuato, and Taxco came into being. Mexico City became the most impressive city in the Americas. All the cities were

The Spaniards built a huge monastery in Huejotzingo in 1529. It is famed for its ornate doorways.

graced with Spanish colonial architecture, a delicate blending of European styles and local materials. Indigenous artists created brilliant statues and wall paintings to adorn the churches. Spanish priests were amazed by their skills.

The Spaniards also found a fortune of untapped gold and silver beneath the ground in Mexico. Some five thousand silver mines operated in New Spain. Indigenous Mexicans, who were virtual slaves, worked the mines under brutal Spanish bosses. The treasures of gold and silver allowed Spain to build a mighty fleet of warships and become a major power in Europe.

The government of New Spain was rigidly controlled by Spanish authorities far across the Atlantic Ocean. Spain made great contributions to Mexico's development. But after three hundred years of living under laws made by people in a distant land, the Mexicans longed for self-government. Beginning in the early 1800s, Mexicans started to whisper an exciting but dangerous word—independence!

On the morning of September 15, 1810, a priest named Miguel Hidalgo y Costilla rang a church bell in the tiny town of Dolores. After the villagers gathered at the church steps, Father Hidalgo did not begin religious services. Instead, he issued a call for revolution. This bold act by a parish priest began the Mexican War of Independence. Hidalgo gathered a huge army of indigenous people, rallying them under the banner of the Virgin of Guadalupe.

Father Hidalgo gives the call to revolution in 1810. Hidalgo was captured and executed in 1811.

Mexican Independence Day

Father Hidalgo launched the Mexican War of Independence at the doorstep of his church in the town of Dolores, about 150 miles (240 km) north of Mexico City. There he made a famous speech—the *"Grito de Dolores"* ("Cry of Dolores")—that spurred the people to action. No one knows his exact words. Today, speakers reenact the speech on the night of September 15 by shouting out *"Viva Hidalgo* ("Long live Hidalgo!")! *"Viva independencia! Viva Mexico!"* Crowds gather at town squares and repeat each chant: "Viva! Viva! Viva!" Fireworks explode, church bells ring, and bands play

the Mexican national anthem. The next day, September 16, is Mexican Independence Day. This joyous day is celebrated with parades and patriotic music.

A New Nation

The War of Independence lasted for eleven years. Finally, Mexicans achieved their dream, but the nation was sadly unprepared for self-government. A long and dismal period of political instability followed. Presidents were changed through army rebellions rather than by free elections.

Political confusion left Mexico vulnerable to its powerful neighbor to the north—the United States. In the early 1800s, Mexico included what is now Texas, New Mexico, Arizona, California, and parts of Nevada, Utah, and Colorado. But the ever-expanding United States wanted those territories. This conflict would lead to war.

For years, Mexico had allowed U.S. settlers to enter Texas. In 1836, the settlers declared Texas to be an independent nation. A battle broke out at an old church called the Alamo

U.S. troops attack Mexico City in 1847. At the end of the Mexican War, Mexico was forced to give the United States all of California, Nevada, and Utah and parts of New Mexico, Arizona, Wyoming, and Colorado.

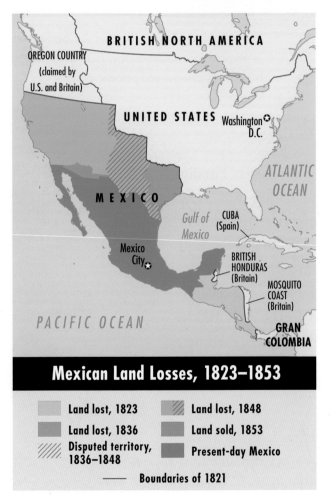

Mexican Land Losses, 1823–1853

- Land lost, 1823
- Land lost, 1836
- Disputed territory, 1836–1848
- Land lost, 1848
- Land sold, 1853
- Present-day Mexico
- —— Boundaries of 1821

in San Antonio, Texas. Mexican troops, led by General Antonio López de Santa Anna, crushed the revolt and killed many Americans holed up in the Alamo. Texas, however, would go on to become independent. Ten years later, the United States went to war under the battle cry, "Remember the Alamo!"

The Mexican War, fought from 1846 to 1848, was a disaster for Mexico. American troops occupied the seaport of Veracruz and marched into Mexico City. As a result of the war, Mexico was forced to hand over its northern territories to the United States. To this day, many Mexicans ponder this incredible loss of land and feel bitter toward their mighty neighbor.

Confusion and civil war continued to plague Mexico after its defeat. In 1853, the United States bought from Mexico a narrow strip of land called the Gadsden Purchase, which now makes up part of southern Arizona and New Mexico. From 1863 to 1867, French troops occupied Mexico. The French installed an archduke from Austria named Maximilian to rule the nation. Maximilian was finally overthrown and replaced by Mexico's legitimate president, Benito Juárez.

The Remarkable Benito Juárez

A Zapotec, Benito Juárez was born into poverty in a small village in the state of Oaxaca. His parents died when he was just three years old, but he still managed to get an education. When he was twelve, he walked into the city of Oaxaca to find a better life for himself. At the time, he could not read or write. But a priest soon noticed Juárez's intelligence and arranged for him to attend school. In time, Juárez became a lawyer and then a judge.

Juárez became president in 1858 while civil war raged in Mexico. As president, he promoted education and tried to reduce the power that the Catholic Church held over the country. He died in office in 1872.

In 1876, General Porfirio Díaz took power in Mexico. Except for a brief period, he ruled for the next thirty years. He led with an iron fist, and he brought an end to army rebellions and civil wars. Díaz tried to modernize Mexico by building railroads and encouraging the expansion of factories.

The Díaz government achieved progress, but the gap between rich and poor grew at an alarming rate. Land ownership became a burning issue. Before the Díaz era, 20 percent of the Mexican people owned at least a small plot of land. By 1910, only 2 percent were landowners. Meanwhile, a handful of wealthy families amassed huge plantations.

Forging Modern Mexico

In late 1910, resentments among many Mexicans boiled over. In the north, rebels waged war under a one-time bandit named Francisco "Pancho" Villa. In the south, the peasant general Emiliano Zapata led landless farmers in hit-and-run attacks against wealthy plantations. Aging President Díaz was forced to leave Mexico. A democratic idealist named Francisco Madero became president, but he could not hold the nation together. Madero was executed by the pro-Díaz army general Victoriano Huerta. With Huerta in power, the great Mexican Revolution erupted.

From 1910 to 1920, civil war swept across Mexico. Rebels fought government forces, and rebel generals fought each other. The Mexican Revolution was the bloodiest war ever fought in the Americas, surpassing even the slaughter of the American Civil War. More than a million Mexicans died in the

Pancho Villa had once been a cattle thief and a bandit. He became a leader of the Mexican Revolution.

fighting. In 1920, the war ended—the exhausted people simply could not fight any longer. Álvaro Obregón stepped up to lead the nation.

Despite the terrible bloodshed, Mexico emerged from the fighting more unified than ever before. Gone were the old class distinctions among whites, indigenous peoples, and mestizos. Now all were Mexicans. A new constitution, written in 1917, separated church from state and guaranteed the rights of workers. In the decades after the revolution, the nation enjoyed an artistic rebirth. Mexican painters became famous throughout the world.

Viva Zapata!

One hero, Emiliano Zapata, rose like a brilliant star from the bloodshed of the Mexican Revolution. Born in the southern state of Morelos, Zapata wanted no power for himself. Instead, he fought for the rights of landless farmers. "Land and liberty" was the battle cry of his followers. Zapata was ambushed and killed in 1919, but many say he defied death itself. For years, people in the south claimed they still saw Zapata riding at night on a gleaming white horse.

A Mexican woman picks cotton in Mississippi. Between 1942 and 1964, more than four million Mexicans went to the United States under the Bracero Program to work as farmhands.

In 1934, a governor named Lázaro Cárdenas became president. Cárdenas was known for his honesty and for promoting education and help for the poor. As president, he began a program of distributing land to peasants who had none. He also had the government take over the oil industry and the electricity industry.

By the time Cárdenas's term ended in 1940, World War II (1939–1945) had already started. During the war, Mexico aided the United States by participating in the Bracero Program (often translated as "helping hand"). The program allowed Mexican farmworkers to come north and help bring in harvests. Thousands of rural Mexicans got their first view of the United States while working as braceros.

After the war, Mexico enjoyed a period of prosperity and political peace. Certainly many Mexicans lived in wretched poverty, but the public school system was now open to all, and Mexico had a wealth of oil to export to other nations.

The country was making such progress that Mexico City was chosen to host the 1968 Summer Olympics. But the nation's advances masked discontent. President Gustavo Díaz Ordaz often dealt harshly with the citizens of his country. Striking workers had been fired, and freedom of speech had been limited. As the Olympics drew near, student protests against government policies increased. Díaz decided to send in the military to break up a protest in Mexico City. The military fired on the protesters, killing hundreds of people. It was an event that shocked the nation.

At the 1968 Mexico City Olympics, Norma Enriqueta Basilio became the first woman to light the Olympic flame. Basilio was a Mexican hurdler.

In the late 1970s, an economic crisis struck Mexico. Inflation spiraled out of control. Almost overnight, the country's currency, the peso, plunged in value. The weakened peso wiped out the savings of the workers. At one time, a working family thought that having a thousand pesos in the bank was a comfortable hedge against sickness or job loss. By the mid-1980s, one thousand pesos—the life savings for many families—was the price of a candy bar.

Armed rebellion emerged again in Mexico during the 1990s. In the southern state of Chiapas, landless Mayan farmers fought pitched battles with the Mexican army. One band of farmers marched under the banner of the revolutionary war hero Emiliano Zapata. Remembering his spirit, the farmers called themselves the Zapatistas.

The Political Revolution

When the Mexican Revolution ended in 1920, one political party rose to capture the country's voters. This was the Institutional Revolutionary Party, or PRI as it is usually called. For seventy years, the PRI ruled without interruption. Rival political parties existed, but they offered only token challenges to the PRI. Some said this dominance by a single party gave the country stability. Others maintained that the PRI denied true democracy to the Mexican people. Candidates for high offices such as the president were chosen in closed-door meetings conducted by PRI officials.

Then the peso crisis and the country's economic slowdown eroded the people's faith in the PRI. In 1988, a popular leader named Cuautémoc Cárdenas (the son of a beloved ex-president) ran for president under a political group called the Party of the Democratic Revolution. Cárdenas lost in a close election. Critics charged that Cárdenas was defeated because of vote fraud committed by PRI bosses. Still, the strong showing of an opposition candidate proved the absolute power of the PRI was broken at last.

Finally, in July 2000, Vicente Fox Quesada of the National Action Party (PAN) won the presidential election. To many Mexicans, this change from a one-party system was a giant step toward real democracy. The 2000 election was the most honest and open election in Mexican history, as candidates from several parties won seats in state and national government.

Mexicans look to future elections with growing excitement. Elections used to be routine because everyone knew the PRI candidates would win. But now, Mexico has enjoyed a political revolution—a revolution accomplished without bloodshed.

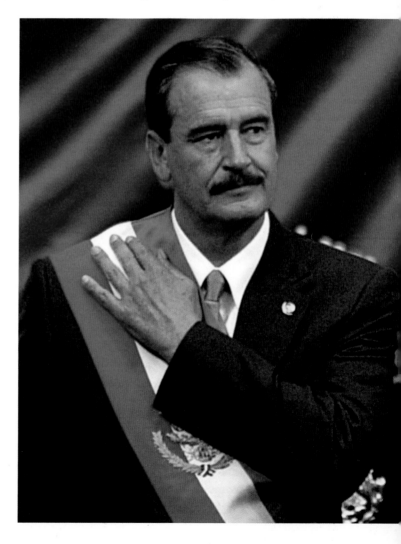

Vicente Fox of the National Action Party was elected president in 2000. Prior to that, the PRI had held the presidency since 1929.

The
Government
of Mexico

Mexico's official name is Estados Unidos Mexicanos (United Mexican States). Like its neighbor to the north, Mexico is divided into states. Each state has its own capital city and enjoys some degree of self-government. Mexico has thirty-one states and one federal district. The federal district surrounds Mexico City, the nation's capital.

The federal government has great power. It raises money through taxes. It can seize land and businesses in the name of the common good. Each state has its own governor and legislature. Under special circumstances, the federal government

Opposite: **A student at the University of Guadalajara. Founded in 1792, it is the second-oldest university in Mexico.**

Mexico City and the surrounding area is home to more than twenty million people. The sprawling city is famed for its traffic problems and its pollution.

can replace a state governor or suspend a state legislature. Towns are governed by a president and a city council. A town or a city can also be taken over by the federal government if federal authorities feel it is necessary to keep the peace. All high officials in the federal and local governments are elected by the people. Any Mexican older than eighteen may vote.

The Structure of Government

The constitution of 1917 spells out the rules for the federal government. The Mexican Constitution divides the nation's government into three departments: the executive, the legislative, and the judicial.

The executive department is headed by the president. His or her job is to enforce the country's laws. The constitution

President Vicente Fox delivers a speech to the National Congress.

President Vicente Fox

In the year 2000, Vicente Fox (shown at right with his daughter) accomplished what many Mexicans thought to be a miracle: he became the first president from a party other than the PRI since 1929. Fox was born to a wealthy family in Mexico City in 1942. When he was a child, his family moved to a farming region in the state of Guanajuato in central Mexico. There he played with the children of poor farmers. He later wrote that he saw "close up one of the evils that unnecessarily afflicted our country: poverty." In 1995, Fox was elected governor of Guanajuato, and he soon had his eye on the presidency. Charming and handsome, he is well liked, even by his political opponents. His wife, Marta Sahagun, is a popular speaker at political rallies, and some speculate she will one day run for high office.

gives the president wide powers to make appointments and to command the armed forces. The president appoints a cabinet to run different sections of the government. Important cabinet posts include the secretary of government and the secretary of finance. The president is elected for one six-year term and cannot run for reelection. There is no vice president. The legislative branch appoints a replacement if the president cannot finish a term.

NATIONAL GOVERNMENT OF MEXICO

Executive Branch

PRESIDENT

CABINET

Legislative Branch

SENATE
(128 MEMBERS)

CHAMBER OF DEPUTIES
(500 MEMBERS)

Judicial Branch

SUPREME COURT OF JUSTICE
(21 MEMBERS)

The legislative department is called the Congress of the Union. It consists of a 128-member Senate and a 500-member Chamber of Deputies. The deputies and senators come from every state in the country. Senators are elected to one six-year term. Deputies serve three-year terms. Deputies can be reelected but cannot serve two terms in a row. The legislature makes the laws for the country.

The judicial department is made up of the court system. The nation's highest court, the Supreme Court of Justice, has twenty-one members. These justices are appointed by the president with the consent of the Senate. Below the Supreme Court are circuit courts and district courts.

The Flag of Mexico

The flag of Mexico is made up of three broad stripes—green, white, and red. The green represents the independence movement from Spain, the white the purity of the Catholic Church, and the red the blood spilled by national heroes. In the center of the flag is an eagle perched on a cactus while eating a snake. This symbol of the eagle and cactus comes from the Aztec legend about the founding of Mexico City.

Getting Around Underground

A modern-day miracle in Mexico City is its subway system, called the Metro. First opened in 1969, the Metro now has ten lines and 176 stations. It serves four million riders a day, making it the third-busiest subway system in the world. Rides on the metro cost only twenty U.S. cents. Subway stations are clean and well lit. The Pino Suárez station is also a museum because when the station was being built, workers digging there uncovered an Aztec temple. Rather than move the temple, Metro engineers simply built a subway station around it. Now commuters waiting for trains gaze at a wonderful relic of the past.

The "Little Bite"

Claudia is a seventeen-year-old who lives in the Yucatán city of Mérida. Like many teenagers, she wanted a driver's license, so she went to her township office to ask for the application papers. A man there told her to see a *licenciado* (legal aide). The licenciado said Claudia must pay him a fee for legal services. Also she had to give him money that he would pass on to a township clerk as a tip. The clerk would issue the driver's license application papers only after receiving the money. This tip, Claudia knew, is called a *mordida*, a "little bite."

Mexico City has one of the highest crime rates in the world. This problem is made worse because many people believe that the police are corrupt, so they do not trust them.

Paying the little bite is an institution in Mexico. If a police officer stops a driver for speeding, the officer will often accept a mordida on the street instead of taking the driver to court. Workers for utility companies sometimes operate under the mordida system. If your telephone is out of service, a mordida to the service person will ensure your phone gets fixed much more quickly. In some towns, even the garbage collectors demand a mordida before they collect the garbage.

Generally, the people collecting the mordidas do not think of themselves as dishonest. They would not dream of stealing money from another person or taking anything from anyone's house. Instead, they look upon mordidas as part of their pay, a harmless fee for services rendered.

The mordida system is part of high government circles as well. There the "little bite" can become a very big bite indeed. In the late 1980s, Mexico City's chief of police lived in a mansion with fifteen bedrooms, five swimming pools, and even a horse-racing track on its grounds. The estate was worth $2.5 million. The chief's official salary was about $65 a month. Clearly, bribery and corruption paid for the chief's grand house.

Mexicans are outraged and disgusted at reports of corruption by their officials and political leaders. Meanwhile, on the streets, they pay the little bite to local police, and life goes on as always.

Mexico's National Anthem

Mexico's national anthem was written in 1854. The words are by Francisco González Bocanegra, and the music is by Jaime Nunó.

CHORUS:

Mexicanos, al grito de guerra
el acero aprestad y el bridón,
y retiemble en sus centros la tierra
al sonoro rugir del cañón.

Ciña ¡oh Patria! tus sienes de oliva
de la paz el arcángel divino;
que en el cielo tu eterno destino
por el dedo de Dios se escribió.
Mas si oscare un extraño enemigo
profaner con su planta tu suelo
piensa ¡oh Patria querida! que el cielo
un soldado en cada hijo te dio.

CHORUS

¡Patria! ¡Patria! tus hijos te juran
exhalar en tus aras su aliento
si el clarín con su bélico acento
los convoca a lidiar con valor.
¡Para ti las guirnaldas de oliva!
¡Un recuerdo para ellos de gloria!
¡Un laurel para ti de victoria!
¡Un sepulcro para ellos de honor!

CHORUS

CHORUS:

Mexicans, at the cry of battle
lend your swords and bridle;
and let the Earth tremble at its center
upon the roar of the cannon.

Your forehead shall be girded,
oh fatherland, with olive garlands by
the divine archangel of peace,
For in heaven your eternal destiny has
been written by the hand of God.
But should a foreign enemy
Profane your land with his sole,
Think, beloved fatherland, that heaven gave you a soldier in each son.

CHORUS

Fatherland, fatherland, your children swear
to exhale their breath in your cause,
if the bugle in its belligerent tone should
call upon them to struggle with bravery.
For you the olive garlands!
For them a memory of glory!
For you a laurel of victory!
For them a tomb of honor!

CHORUS

El Norte

Mexicans have a saying: "Poor Mexico; so far from God, so close to the United States." Mexico is a developing country where masses of people live in poverty. Yet the richest country on earth lies just to the north across a long, thin border. This situation creates special problems in the lives of Mexicans.

The United States is called *El Norte* (the north) by the Mexican people. Their powerful neighbor is respected, but also resented. Many Mexicans regard the United States as a schoolyard bully that has sometimes enjoyed beating up on the weaker country next door. No one has forgotten the Mexican-American War, which cost Mexico almost half its territory. As recently as 1914, during the Mexican Revolution, U.S. troops occupied the port city of Veracruz.

The border between the United States and Mexico runs for 1,945 miles (3,130 km). A fence separates the two countries along part of the border.

The border between the United States and Mexico stretches close to 2,000 miles (3,200 km). At border cities such as Tijuana and Ciudad Juárez, children learn English by watching cartoons broadcast from the United States. Dollars are exchanged freely in the stores along with pesos.

Mexican families wade across the Rio Grande to get into the United States. More than a million people sneak across the border each year.

The border is well defined by the Rio Grande along Texas and much of New Mexico. But farther west, a land border stretches all the way to the Pacific Ocean. There are many spots along this border where illegal immigrants or drug smugglers can cross undetected. Drug smuggling is an explosive problem facing the two countries. It is estimated that two-thirds of the illegal drugs entering the United States are brought in from Mexico. Not all the drugs are manufactured in Mexico. Drug traffickers often bring drugs into Mexico from other nations and then smuggle them across the border.

Despite frequent squabbles, Mexico's relations with the United States are good. In 2000, 8.8 million people living in the United States had been born in Mexico, and an additional 20 million Americans were of Mexican heritage. These figures mean the two countries are more than just neighbors. In many ways, the United States and Mexico are family.

Mexico City: A Place of Legends

A legend says the Aztecs once lived in a well-watered, fertile land called Aztlan. Somehow, the people displeased a powerful god. The god expelled them from the paradise of Aztlan, and the Aztecs wandered the deserts of northern Mexico for hundreds of years. Another god told them to seek out a place where they would see an eagle perched on a cactus while eating a snake. There they must build a grand city. Tradition says the Aztecs saw the eagle vision in the year 1325. Obeying their god, they constructed a city and called it Tenochtitlán, meaning "place of the cactus." The Aztecs believed their city, founded by the order of a god, was a place of magic.

The capital, now called Mexico City, was built in the exact spot where Tenochtitlán once stood. Many Mexicans believe the magic of the place remains to this day. In the center of the city is a broad plaza called the Zócalo. It was there that the wandering Aztecs were supposed to have seen the eagle devouring a snake. In Aztec times, the city's two tallest pyramids stood at the plaza. The National Cathedral (above), the country's most important church, now rises on the Zócalo's north end. Also flanking the Zócalo is the National Palace, the site of the president's offices.

The Zócalo remains the spiritual and political center of Mexico. Young couples come here to get married, believing this sacred ground will cement their bonds throughout their lives. In recent years, the Zócalo has been the center of political firestorms. Workers gather in the square to hold noisy demonstrations. There is no better place to hold a rally than in the historic center of Mexico City.

Beyond the Zócalo, Mexico City streets burst with life. Street vendors are everywhere, sitting by the curb selling everything from candy bars to computers. Tree-lined boulevards cut through the heart of the city. High-rise apartment buildings along these boulevards house the rich and the superrich. The poor live in slum districts in the northern section.

Parks are the respite of this overcrowded and traffic-choked city. Grandest of all is Chapultepec Park (right). Once the private hunting grounds for Aztec noblemen, Chapultepec is now the city's favorite playground. About one million people visit the park each Sunday. Situated in Chapultepec Park is the Museum of Anthropology, one of the world's great showcases of ancient cultures.

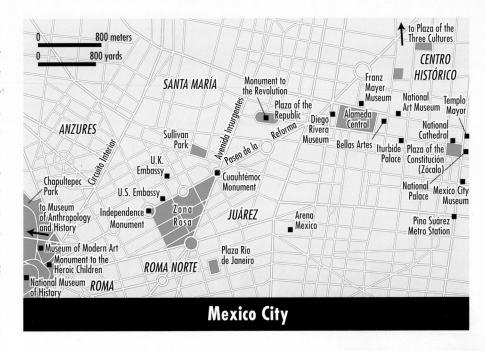

Mexico City

The Economic Struggle

THE CITY OF MONTERREY IS ONE OF MEXICO'S LEADING industrial centers. Monterrey has more than five hundred factories producing items ranging from concrete and steel products to clothing and soft drinks. Factories in the city employ thousands of workers. Yet the streets of Monterrey are filled with people who shine shoes, sell newspapers, or wash car windows for a living. Most of the street vendors would prefer to have a steady job in a factory, but such openings are rare. Monterrey reflects the troubles faced by Mexico's economy: there are far more workers than there are jobs.

Opposite: **A woman working in Mexico City carries a load of bricks.**

Monterrey is filled with factories like this salt plant.

Fire-Eaters

Mexico City is filled with street entertainers such as musicians and magicians. The most spectacular of the entertainers are young men called *tragafuegos* (fire-eaters). The fire-eaters appear at twilight carrying a can of gasoline and a flaming torch made from a bent-up coat hanger with cloth wrapped around its tip. They put gasoline in their mouths, hold the torch a few inches from their lips, and blow out, sending a finger of flame into the air. The young men are burning their lungs to ashes hoping to collect a few coins from the crowds who watch their acts. Laws have been passed banning the tragafuegos, but they keep reappearing. Earning a living is always difficult for the young in Mexico City. Many people, like the tragafuegos, do whatever they can to make some money.

Mexico has a young population. Almost half the nation's people are under twenty years old. Every year, about a million young people reach working age and begin to look for jobs. But even in good times, job growth does not keep up with population growth.

True unemployment figures are difficult to compile. When Mexicans have no steady job, they work as helpers on delivery trucks or even as scavengers in garbage dumps. Because these self-employed workers have some means of earning money, the government does not consider them unemployed.

The Lure of the North

A semiskilled worker in a Monterrey factory earns the equivalent of about eight dollars a day. A few hundred miles to the north, in the United States, factories pay eight dollars an hour for the same work. It is no wonder that Mexicans long to go to El Norte to work.

Each year, the United States accepts more immigrants from Mexico than from any other country. Still, the wait for legal immigration can take many years. Desperate people feel they cannot wait. Between 1990 and 2002, illegal immigration from Mexico increased 66 percent. Some people say that as many as three million people illegally crossed the U.S.–Mexico border in 2004 alone. Not all of these people

Mexicans sneaking across the border face a long, hard trip. They must pass through large swaths of dry, empty land where finding food and water is difficult.

were Mexican. Many people entered Mexico from other Latin American countries or from Asia or Africa and then slipped over the border into the United States.

Most illegal Mexican immigrants to the United States are men who find jobs, live frugally, and send money back to their families. Money sent from workers in the United States is the second- or third-largest source of income for the Mexican people. Although U.S. authorities call them illegals, the workers do not believe they are breaking a law. To them, sneaking across the border is an economic issue. They wish to work, and the best jobs are in the United States.

The illegals return to Mexico for holidays or when they are feeling terribly lonely for their families. After a brief visit, they return to El Norte. They cross by wading the Rio Grande, by hiking at night through a lonely desert, by paying a professional smuggler (called a coyote), or by hiding in a boxcar or in the back of a truck. Sneaking across the border can be dangerous. Immigrants freeze to death when the temperatures drop or die from a lack of water in the broiling desert. Some are murdered by gangs that attack them for their meager savings. An estimated 2,500 illegals died during the 1990s while making the trek across the border.

Business owners in the United States know that Mexicans, whether they are legal or illegal immigrants, are hard workers. They are willing to take difficult, low-paying jobs that are often shunned by U.S. citizens. Mexicans pick cotton under the hot Texas sun. They wash dishes in the steamy kitchens of restaurants. Many are skilled bricklayers, carpenters, or electricians. Whatever their jobs, Mexicans generally perform well and make few complaints. The illegals cannot complain to the government about dangerous working conditions because in the eyes of the government, they are criminals with no protection under the law.

Jobs and Resources

In 1994, Canada, the United States, and Mexico signed the North American Free Trade Agreement (NAFTA). The agreement cut tariffs, or taxes, on goods shipped among the three countries. Many workers in the United States opposed NAFTA. They argued that now factory owners would buy parts made by low-paid Mexican workers and then fire higher-paid factory workers in the United States. Without a doubt, the passage of NAFTA has created thousands of new factory jobs in Mexico. How many jobs NAFTA has cost north of the border is still a matter of debate.

Workers make shoes at a factory in León. León has long been the center of shoe production in Mexico.

Even before the passage of NAFTA, huge factories were built in Mexico along the U.S. border. These factories, called *maquiladores*, were established to take advantage of the lower wages paid in Mexico. Most of the maquiladores are owned by U.S. companies. Workers in the border plants manufacture car parts and assemble computers and television sets. The final products are often sold in the United States. By the mid-1990s, more than two thousand maquiladores along the border employed about five hundred thousand Mexican workers. In recent years, some border factories have moved their operations to China, India, and Indonesia, where wages are even lower than in Mexico.

About 50 percent of Mexican workers are employed in the service industries. These are industries that provide services rather than make products. Schoolteachers, store clerks, and accountants at a bank are all service workers. Mexico's largest single employer is the retail giant Wal-Mart, which runs 664 stores in sixty-six Mexican cities and employs more than one hundred thousand men and women.

A teacher leads a class at a school in Mexico City. Education is one of Mexico's large service industries.

Tourism creates service jobs in hotels and restaurants. Mexico has a pleasant climate, friendly people, sparkling beaches, and fascinating ruins. For these reasons, millions of visitors come to the sunny country each year. In 2003, a record 9.2 million tourists arrived in Mexico and spent $9.5 billion. Mexico now ranks tenth in the world in terms of tourism income.

Tourists admire the Mayan ruins at Chichén Itzá. It is the most visited site in the Yucatán.

A boy works in a cornfield in the Yucatán Peninsula. Corn is a staple of the Mexican diet, and many families grow it for their own use.

Only 12 percent of Mexico's total land area is used for farming. Rocky soil and poor rainfall make most of the land unsuitable for crops. The best farmland is found in the southern half of the Plateau of Mexico. In the southern lowlands, rain is plentiful, but inadequate drainage turns the land into soggy marshes. Corn is the major crop throughout the country. Corn is used to make tortillas, the common bread of Mexico. Other important crops include bananas, cotton, lemons, mangoes, and oranges.

What Mexico Grows, Makes, and Mines

Agriculture (2002)

Sugarcane	45,635,000 metric tons
Corn	19,299,000 metric tons
Sorghum	5,206,000 metric tons

Manufacturing (2001, value in Mexican pesos)

Machinery and equipment	95, 497,400,000
Telecommunications and sound equipment	19,142,200,000
Office machines	13,188,400,000

Mining (2002)

Silver	2,852,138 metric tons
Zinc	391,711 metric tons
Copper	308,388 metric tons

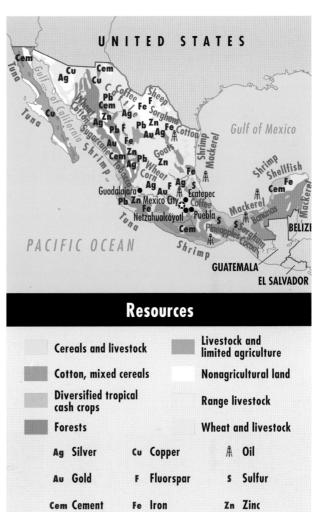

Resources

Cereals and livestock	Livestock and limited agriculture
Cotton, mixed cereals	Nonagricultural land
Diversified tropical cash crops	Range livestock
Forests	Wheat and livestock

Ag	Silver	Cu	Copper	⚒	Oil
Au	Gold	F	Fluorspar	s	Sulfur
Cem	Cement	Fe	Iron	Zn	Zinc

Oil is a billion-dollar industry in Mexico, Latin America's leading oil producer. But oil production does not generate large numbers of jobs. Mexico ranks as the world's leading silver producer. About one-sixth of the world's annual production of silver comes from Mexico. Copper, gold, lead, salt, and zinc are also taken from Mexico's mines.

Above left: **The government runs the oil industry in Mexico. The oil and gas industry account for about one-third of the government's income.**

Rich and Poor—A Widening Gap

About 70 percent of Mexico's people live in poverty, and half of those live in dreadful conditions. Many poor families earn less than $135 a month. But other Mexican families go out to elegant restaurants and spend $100 on dinner alone. Sometimes the wealthy people make an after-dinner toast. They clink glasses and say, "To Mexico, still the best country in the world to be rich in."

To be rich in Mexico means having maids, cooks, and a driver to pick up the children from school. The rich can surround themselves with servants because they pay low wages. Mexico's rich include lawyers, bankers, doctors, and politicians. There are also the superrich, whose families have owned the best land and the most productive mines for generations. Some reports say that about half the nation's wealth is controlled by two dozen large family groups.

Mexico's Currency

The peso is the basic unit of Mexican currency. It is divided into one hundred centavos. In the 1980s, the peso's value went wild and traded as high as three thousand to the dollar. This currency crisis led to terrible inflation, which destroyed the savings of the middle class. Today, the peso is stable. In 2006, ten pesos equaled about one U.S. dollar. The most common coin used in Mexico is worth ten pesos. Bills start at twenty pesos and go up to five hundred pesos. The bills feature a picture of a historic figure on the front. Benito Juárez is on the twenty-peso note.

The Minimum Wage

Mexico has a minimum wage, a rate of pay that employers cannot dip below. In 2005, the minimum wage in Mexico City was forty-five pesos a day. This is little more than the cost of a Big Mac, large fries, and a shake at one of the city's many McDonald's restaurants. Most people earn more than the minimum wage, but many city residents struggle to survive on forty-five pesos a day.

In the 1960s and the 1970s, a strong middle class developed in Mexico. The middle class was made up of small-business owners, farmers, and schoolteachers. These were educated, hardworking people who looked forward to a bright future. Then inflation erased the savings of middle-class people. Gone were the dreams of sending children to college, expanding a business, or building a nicer house. Many middle-class Mexicans never recovered from the wild inflation.

Mexico's poor people have little sympathy for the middle class who are having trouble keeping up. The poor consider the middle class to be wealthy. Irene Beatriz Navarro, a thirty-year-old mother of three, works as a maid. "I don't see [the middle class] suffering," she says. "They have nannies. They also have a cook and a washerwoman. I know because I am all those things." Navarro was fired one early December from her housecleaning job. She suspects she was dismissed because her boss did not want to pay her a Christmas bonus. "How can I try harder?" Navarro asks. "How? I already try as hard as I can."

Many middle-class people in Mexico hire maids to keep their houses clean.

CHAPTER SEVEN

A Look at the People

Many Mexican cities hold parades on the Día de la Raza.

IN MEXICO, COLUMBUS DAY—OCTOBER 12—IS CALLED *Día de la Raza* (Day of the Race). Christopher Columbus is honored because his voyage led to the development of the mestizo people, by far the largest ethnic group in Mexico today. It is a bittersweet holiday, however. The mestizo people, called *la raza* (the race), were born out of war and conquest. Today, no one knows exact numbers of the mestizo population. At one time, the Mexican government kept a census dividing the people into three categories: mestizos, indigenous people, and whites. No such survey with racial categorization has been taken since the 1920s. The U.S. government, however, estimates that 60 percent of Mexicans are mestizo.

Opposite: A young girl wears an elaborate costume at a festival in Merida.

Blacks in Mexico

Slavery was permitted in Mexico during the three hundred years it was known as New Spain. Under Spanish rule, about two hundred thousand African slaves were taken to Mexico. Long ago, blacks merged into the Mexican population. Today, blacks from the United States and other countries claim they get curious stares when visiting remote regions of Mexico because the people are simply not accustomed to seeing black people.

A Mayan boy harvests tomatoes. Indigenous people make up a majority of the population in Chiapas, Oaxaca, and parts of the Yucatán.

Determining the racial breakdown of Mexico is further complicated because people do not agree on who is an indigenous person or *indígena*, as they are known in Mexico. In many respects, being indígena is a state of mind and a lifestyle. Indígenas are defined as people who live in a predominantly indigenous area and who use indigenous phrases in their speech. Mestizos or whites can be considered indígena under this loose definition.

There is a huge variation in how Mexicans look. Some Mexicans are blonds who look like they might very well be natives of Denmark. The features of the Maya have not changed since before Spanish times. Mexico is in every respect a multiracial society. Yet one group—the dark-skinned mestizo—is the majority.

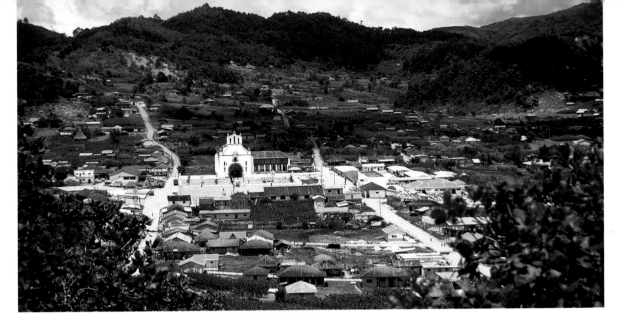

In San Juan Chamula, the Maya still practice many of their ancient traditions.

The Güeros

Look at the comedies on Mexican television. The shows are often about white, middle-class families. Then look at the TV advertisements. The woman who claims her favorite brand of detergent performs miracles on her dishes is white. The little boy praising a dessert is light-skinned and blond. Ask a Mexican why white people play such a prominent role on TV programs and you get mixed replies. Many will shrug their shoulders and say, "Well, the advertisers want to sell their products"—meaning, if white people buy the detergent, it must be good.

Ethnic Mexico

Mestizo	60%
Indigenous	30%
Caucasian	9%
Other	1%

The Indigenous Way of Life

Mexico's indigenous people tend to be concentrated in certain regions. In some places, indígenas practice the old ways and exist almost as a separate society within Mexico. One such area is the southern state of Chiapas, along the border with Guatemala. The people there, mostly Maya, blend ancient religious customs with Catholicism. Chiapan men and women chant traditional prayers in front of the statues of Catholic saints. But many Maya, especially older people, also leave the saints special gifts. Sometimes they place a few eggs or a soft drink at the foot of the statues. Hundreds of years ago, the Maya regularly gave presents to the statues of their gods in hopes of winning their favor.

Mexicans use the word *güeros* to describe white people. Güeros are thought to be handsome, lucky, and rich. There is some truth to equating whiteness with wealth. Hundreds of years ago, white-skinned Spaniards and other Europeans seized Mexico's best farmland and its most productive mines. Whites tended to marry other whites, so for centuries the wealth remained with light-skinned families.

To this day, white or light-skinned Mexicans are usually wealthier than mestizos or indígenas. Yet more than money is attached to the image of the güero. Whiteness in Mexico is a standard of beauty. This is especially true for a güera, a light-skinned woman.

Officially, Mexicans praise their indigenous past and honor the mestizo race. Still, when a light-skinned baby is born to a mestizo family, everyone rejoices. Ask why they are happy and they'll say, "This baby will prosper because life is so much easier for whites."

Spanish, the National Language

Almost five hundred years ago, the Spanish conquerors brought their language to what is now Mexico. Before the conquest, dozens of indigenous tongues were spoken in the land. The Spanish language helped to unify the nation, although many people preferred their old languages. Today, Spanish is the official language of Mexico. Almost all Mexicans speak Spanish.

Some older Mexicans use indigenous languages at home, but they speak Spanish on the streets or in the marketplace.

Mexico's Gifts to the Spanish Language

In the Americas, Spaniards came across foods they had never seen before. The words for these new foods went directly from the indigenous languages into Spanish. *Jitomate* (hee-to-MAH-teh) for "tomato" and *cacahuate* (cah-cah-WAH-teh) for "peanut" are examples. The word for one animal—coyote—is pronounced nearly the same in the Náhuatl dialect, Spanish, and English.

Children in such families often grow up believing there is something sinister about indigenous languages. Their mothers and fathers speak the old tongue when they do not want the children to follow their conversation. A small percentage of Mexicans in remote areas use indigenous languages more frequently than they use Spanish. Prominent languages still spoken include Mayan, Náhuatl—the language of the Aztecs—and Zapotec.

Some Spanish words or phrases are used differently in Mexico than in other countries. For example, the Mexican word for "matches" is *cerillos*, meaning "wax." In most other Spanish-speaking countries, "matches" are *fósforos*. "To chat"

Speaking Spanish

The way Spanish words are pronounced closely follows their spellings. A key to pronouncing Spanish is to learn the five vowel sounds: *a* as in father, *e* as in met, *i* as in magazine, *o* as in over, and *u* as in June. Here are a few common words and phrases:

Good	*Bueno* (BWEH-noh)
How are you?	*¿Cómo está usted?* (KOH-moh es-TAH u-STED)
Thank you	*Gracias* (GRAH-syahs)
Please	*Por favor* (pohr fah-VOHR)
What time is it?	*¿Qué hora es?* (keh OHR-ah ehs)

in Mexico is *platicar*, whereas in Spain "to chat" is *charlar*. Although some words are used differently, Mexicans can speak with people in any other Spanish-speaking country.

The Rush to the Cities

The majority of Mexicans live in big cities, and the biggest of all is the capital. How large is Mexico City? Greater Mexico City is home to more people than the combined total of all of Mexico's neighbors to the south: Guatemala, El Salvador, Honduras, Belize, and Nicaragua. Until recently, an accurate census of the city was difficult to take because people were moving in at the rate of three thousand to five thousand a day. In 2004, Mexico City and its suburbs had a population of 21.5 million, making it the third-largest metropolitan area in the world. Almost 25 percent of Mexico's population lives in or near the capital.

The expansion of Mexico City and its metropolitan area is a recent development. In the 1970s, people from the country moved to vacant land in the capital so quickly they were called "parachutists" because it seemed they simply dropped out of

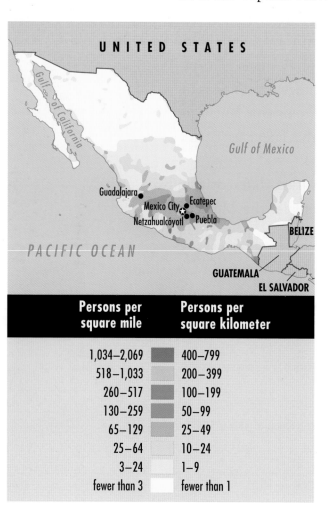

Persons per square mile		Persons per square kilometer
1,034–2,069		400–799
518–1,033		200–399
260–517		100–199
130–259		50–99
65–129		25–49
25–64		10–24
3–24		1–9
fewer than 3		fewer than 1

the sky. The newcomers came to the capital in search of jobs. Nearly one-third of the nation's industrial plants are located in the Mexico City region.

Many thousands of country people settled on a cactus-strewn wasteland that lies on the capital's outskirts. This area has the Aztec name Netzahualcóyotl. Residents there built houses out of scrap bricks, wood, and cardboard. Roofs were fashioned from flattened tin cans hammered together. In just three decades, this collection of huts and shanties grew to become one of Mexico's largest cities.

In 1950, just three million people lived in the Mexico City area. Today, more than twenty million people live there.

A haze often hangs over Mexico City. The persistent pollution can cause breathing difficulties and burning eyes.

Mexico's Population Growth

Year	Population
1940	19,654,000
1950	25,791,000
1960	34,923,000
1970	48,225,000
1980	66,847,000
1990	81,140,922
2000	97,361,711
2004	104,959,594

Netzahualcóyotl is a success story of sorts. Mexicans are brilliant at making the best of what little they have. As the suburb grew, the residents built parks and planted trees along the streets. One by one, families tore down their old shacks and replaced them with cinderblock houses. Homeowners cleared space to plant gardens. They put flowers in window boxes. Netzahualcóyotl no longer has the look of a slum. People living there affectionately call it Netza.

Mexico City's wild growth also has downsides, particularly air pollution. The capital and its suburbs are home to thirty thousand factories and almost three million motor vehicles. All together, more than eleven thousand tons of gaseous wastes pour into the air each day. Because Mexico City is ringed by mountains, the pollutants cannot escape. On windless days, the air is so thick with smog that it is difficult to see even across the street. Mexico City residents frequently suffer from asthma and eye infections. Many experts claim the capital has the most poisonous air of any city in the world.

But solving the problem is difficult, if not impossible. One engineer said that trying to reduce the city's pollution is like trying to "fix an airplane while it's in flight."

All Mexican cities have experienced runaway growth in the last forty years. This is partly because Mexico has one of the world's fastest-growing populations. Between 1950 and 2000, the number of Mexicans increased fourfold. The growth of cities also occurred because of changes in the rural economy in the 1960s and 1970s. Big farmers bought tractors and other equipment, so they didn't need as many farmhands. Also, many small farmers sold their land to large farms. The decrease in farm jobs forced workers to migrate to the cities.

In 1900, only about 10 percent of Mexicans lived in cities and towns. Today, almost 80 percent are city dwellers. In recent years, the Mexican birthrate has slowed, so the population is not increasing at the same pace. The average number of children in a Mexican family has dropped from more than 6 to 2.5. Also, fewer families are making the dash from farms to cities. But Mexico—once a country of farmers—is now solidly an urban society, and the cities are bursting at their seams.

Mexico's Largest Cities

Mexico City	8,591,309
Guadalajara	1,647,720
Ecatepec	1,620,303
Puebla	1,346,176
Netzahualcóyotl	1,224,924

Mexico's birth rate has declined in recent years. But the country's population is still expected to double in thirty-six years.

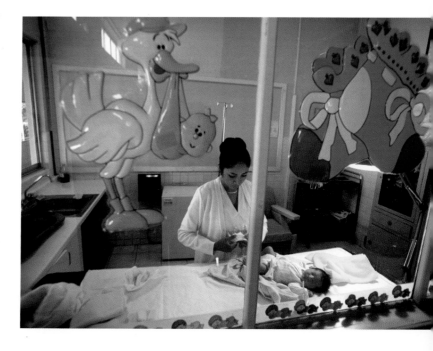

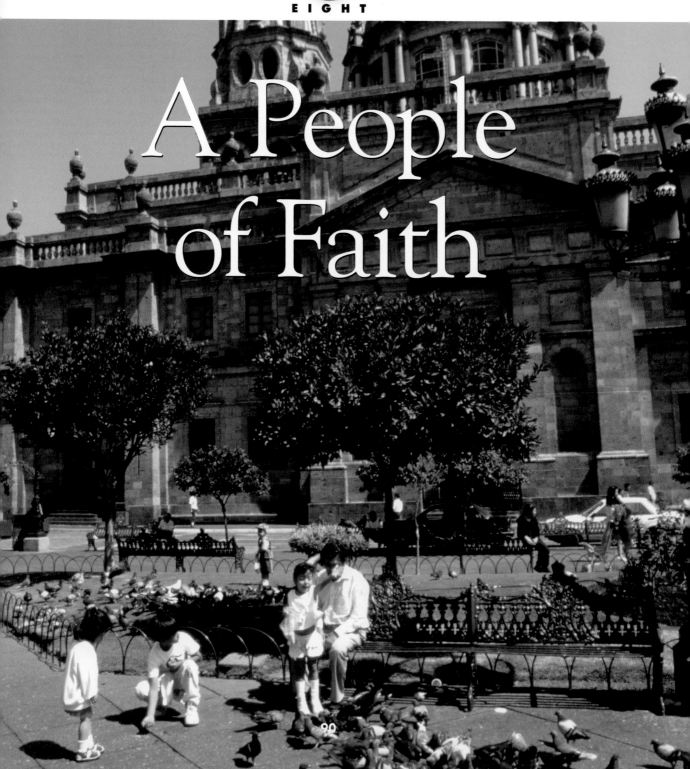

A People
of Faith

R IDE A BUS ANYWHERE IN MEXICO AND YOU WILL NOTICE a hush when the bus passes a church. The riders stop chattering and silently make the sign of the cross—a hand gesture from forehead to chest, left shoulder to right shoulder. People walking on the street also cross themselves in front of a church. Even some drivers stop their cars to perform this ritual—and create a traffic jam in the process. Religion is central to the lives of many Mexicans.

Opposite: **Guadalajara's cathedral takes up an entire city block.**

Many Mexicans stop in at churches to pray even when no services are being held.

About 90 percent of Mexicans are Roman Catholic, and most are resistant to changing churches. In recent years, Mormons, Episcopalians, and other groups have sent ministers to Mexico in hopes of winning converts. The ministers walk door to door talking to people. Officially, they are welcome in the country. Still, many families have posted signs on their doors that politely but firmly inform the missionaries that they do not wish to talk. The signs say: "This household is Catholic. We do not accept propaganda from other faiths."

The National Cathedral

Mexico's largest church is the National Cathedral, which rises in the heart of Mexico City. A huge Aztec pyramid and temple once stood on the very grounds the cathedral now occupies. The present church was built between 1718 and 1737. The Spanish conquerors had built an earlier Catholic church on the same spot. Through the years, the National Cathedral has been raked by bullets during battles and rattled by earthquakes. Still, the ornate church stands proudly and remains the symbol of Mexican Catholicism.

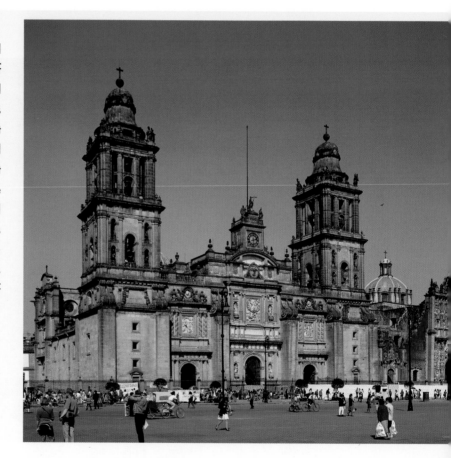

Carnival is one of the most colorful festivals in Mexico. It is a time for wild parties and fabulous parades.

The church and its rituals govern the rhythm of Mexican life. The wild celebration of Carnival begins in February or March. At Carnival parties, people dance and stuff themselves with their favorite foods. Then comes the solemn forty-day period of Lent that leads up to Easter. During Lent, Catholics shun favorite foods and other pleasures. Good Friday, the Friday before Easter, commemorates the day Jesus was killed. In Mexican towns, Good Friday begins with a procession. Slowly, church members carry religious statues and banners through streets lined with people. Many of the onlookers mouth silent prayers or weep as they ponder Christ's sufferings on the cross. On Easter Sunday, however, the somber mood is lifted. On this day, Christ is supposed to have risen from the dead. People celebrate with music, feasting, and laughter.

Religions of Mexico

Roman Catholic	89.7%
Protestant	4.9%
Jewish	0.1%
Other	2.1%
None	3.2%

A People of Faith   **93**

The celebration of Christmas goes on for much of December and into January. It begins in the middle of the month with Las Posadas, which recalls Jesus's parents trying to find a room to stay in before he was born. The celebration of Las Posadas features candlelit processions through town as people reenact the journey. Christmas Day is a time for staying home with family and feasting. Traditionally in Mexico, gift giving took place on January 6, Three Kings Day. This is the day that the Three Wise Men are supposed to have brought gifts to the baby Jesus. Today most children also receive presents on Christmas.

Guadalupe, the Savior of Mexico

At the beginning of December, highways leading to Mexico City become clogged, not only with cars and trucks, but also with people on foot. Hikers—miles and miles of them—stream toward the capital. They are pilgrims coming to celebrate Guadalupe Day on December 12. On that day more than 450 years ago, the picture of the Virgin of Guadalupe supposedly appeared on the straw coat of Juan Diego, an indigenous peasant.

Every year on Guadalupe Day, more than a million people visit the church that holds the picture. For the last mile or so, some pilgrims inch toward the church on their knees, scraping their skin bloody in the process. Some worshippers are dressed in rags. Others wear suits and dresses worth more than the average factory worker earns in a year. The differences between rich and poor, mestizo and indígena melt at the doorway of this special church. As they approach the church, people hold up signs with special messages. One woman held a sign saying, "My family wishes to thank the Virgin for answering our prayers and curing my baby daughter of fever."

Pilgrims on their knees make their way toward the Basilica of Guadalupe. Guadalupe Day is the most important religious holiday in Mexico.

Sister Juana Inés de la Cruz

Juana Inés de la Cruz was born near Mexico City in 1651. By the age of eight, she was writing poetry, poring over classical literature, and amazing scholars with her knowledge of science. While still a teenager, Juana Inés de la Cruz became a nun. She disturbed the powerful priests by writing that the study of science confirms—rather than refutes—the teachings of the Bible. The priests confined her to a cell. According to one legend, she continued writing, using her own blood as ink. During an outbreak of the deadly disease cholera, she refused to leave the convent. Instead, she chose to stay and treat sick nuns. She herself died of cholera in 1695. To this day, Sister Juana Inés de la Cruz is revered in Mexico for her courage.

A new church was built in the 1970s to hold the celebrated painting of the Virgin. Inside the church, worshippers are whisked past the painting on a moving sidewalk. There is no other way to accommodate the masses of people who wish to glimpse the portrait in its golden frame.

The Day of the Dead

Octavio Paz, one of Mexico's foremost philosophers and writers, often wrote about the Mexican character. He puzzled over the people's curious mixture of European and indigenous influences. In one book, Paz discusses the Mexicans' unique attitude toward death: "The word 'death' is not pronounced in New York, in Paris, in London, because it burns the lips. The

Mexican, in contrast, is familiar with death, jokes about it. . . . True [he fears death], but at least death is not hidden away: he looks at it face to face, with impatience, disdain, or irony."

Mexican religious thinking holds that death, like life, is a natural force. This is demonstrated during the Day of the Dead on November 2. The Day of the Dead is a combination of Halloween and All Souls' Day and All Saints' Day, two religious holidays that recall people who have died. The Halloween aspect is the most obvious. Pictures of playful-looking ghosts appear in store windows. Vendors sell sugary

Well-dressed skeletons on display for the Day of the Dead. This celebration mixes joy and death.

Religious Holidays

Three Kings Day	January 6
Carnival	Late February/early March
Easter Week	March or April
Day of the Dead	November 1 and 2
Guadalupe Day	December 12
Christmas	December 25

candy shaped like skulls. Children draw a picture of a skull on a shoe box and cut out holes for eyes and a mouth. On the night of November 1, young people burn a candle in the shoe-box skull and go trick-or-treating. Instead of saying "trick or treat," though, Mexican children chant, "Won't you cooperate with the skull?"

On the morning of November 2, family groups have a picnic at the cemetery. The cemetery may seem an odd place for such a family gathering, but not on the Day of the Dead. First, the families gather at the grave of a

On the Day of the Dead, Mexicans bring flowers to cemeteries to brighten up the graves of their relatives.

Many families bring marigolds to cemeteries on the Day of the Dead. The flowers' orange color is believed to guide the souls to their homes.

relative. They clean the grave, plant some flowers, and say prayers. There is nothing sad about this occasion. It is a time to remember the departed and bring him or her a little cheer. If the dead person liked a particular song, the family sings that song. They also place a banana, a cupcake, a bottle of soda, or some other food on the grave as an offering.

Mexican calendars are dotted with holidays. There is Mail Carriers' Day, a day on which everyone offers food and drink to the person delivering the mail on their route. On Teachers' Day, all students are expected to bring candy or flowers to their teacher. So why not hold a holiday for people in the next world? The Day of the Dead is perfectly natural and a special time of celebration.

Mexicans at Ease

In August 2004, a strange hush gripped Mexico. For more than a week, Mexicans had been following the Olympic Games in Athens, Greece. No Mexican athlete had yet won a medal, meaning none had finished first, second, or third in any event. But now came the women's 400-meter race, where the Mexican runner Ana Guevara was favored to win. Streets emptied as people crowded around television sets to watch the event. The starting gun sounded. Guevara and the other athletes flew down the track. At the last second, a runner from the Bahamas edged in front to win the gold. Ana Guevara finished second, capturing the silver medal. She had performed brilliantly, but Mexicans dreamed of gold. "Poor Ana," said a government official. "No, poor country. Poor Mexico."

Mexico is a sports-mad nation. Sports stories dominate the newspapers and the TV. Sports heroes are treated like kings and queens.

In Mexico, *fútbol* (soccer) is easily the country's favorite team sport. Schools have teams and leagues. In

Opposite: **Members of a traditional dance company perform in Cancún.**

Ana Guevara did not lose a single 400 m race between 2001 and 2004.

Soccer, the Ancient Game

Europeans brought the modern game of soccer to Mexico. But long before Europeans arrived, the peoples of ancient Mexico played a game similar to soccer. The players on two teams tried to get a large rubber ball into the opposing team's goal by pushing it with their hips. The competition was serious. The captain of the winning team was allowed to cut off the head of the losing team's captain!

remote farm areas, kids play against each other on rocky fields where a pair of cacti serve as goalposts.

Mexico's second-leading team sport is *béisbol* (baseball). The game was brought to Mexico from the United States in

Soccer is the most popular sport in Mexico, and around the world. Everyone can play soccer because it requires no special equipment—all that is needed is a ball.

Bobby Avila was the first Mexican to make it big in Major League Baseball in the United States. He led the American League in batting in 1954, hitting .341.

the early 1900s. The language of Mexican baseball is a mixture of English and Spanish. A batter is a *bateador*, a pitcher a *pitchador*, and a shortstop is, well, a shortstop. While baseball is a gift from the north, Mexico has repaid the favor by sending many players to the major leagues in the United States and Canada.

Basketball is becoming increasingly popular in Mexico.

Basketball is a city game in Mexico. Courts are available in most city parks. Mexico's gentle climate allows outdoor basketball to be played year-round. Football, the type played in the United States, is enjoying growing popularity. The game is called *fútbol Americano*. The U.S. style of football would draw greater interest if it were not for the equipment the players must wear. Few Mexican schools can afford to buy helmets, shoulder pads, and the other protective gear needed to play the rough game.

Runners and Walkers

Mexican racewalkers have had surprising success in the Olympic Games. Racewalking was unknown in Mexico until 1968. That year, the Olympics were in Mexico City—the only time they have been held in Latin America. At the 1968 Olympics, a Mexican soldier shocked the racewalking world by capturing a bronze medal. Since then, Mexican walkers have won several gold medals in the Olympic Games. Mexico's best distance runners are the Tarahumara of the Copper Canyon. The Tarahumara are in the habit of running wherever they go. When hunting a deer, they run the animal into exhaustion. The Tarahumara think most organized races—including the 26.2-mile (42 km) marathon—are too short.

Individual sports enjoyed in Mexico include boxing, wrestling, tennis, track and field, and golf. Many Mexicans believe the greatest of these is boxing. Boxing, at all levels, excites fans in Mexico. Small villages bring out a ring, erect lights in a farmer's field, and hold an amateur night. In Mexico City, thousands crowd the Arena Mexico to watch the fights. This love of boxing has reaped rewards. In matches around the world, three groups have won the most gold medals and championships: Americans, Cubans, and Mexicans.

A Boxing Legend

Pound for pound, one of the best boxers in modern times is Mexico's own Julio César Chávez. Over his career, Chávez won more victories than any other lightweight in boxing history. He once went eighty-nine matches without a defeat. Chávez is so popular that Mexican presidential candidates seek his endorsement.

Bullfighting

The word *machismo* describes a type of manly—indeed, super-manly—behavior. A "macho" man will not back down from a street fight, even if his opponent is a head taller and outweighs him by 50 pounds (20 kilograms). Critics of Mexican society claim that most Mexican men act in a macho manner. Defenders say this is nonsense and that only a tiny percentage of Mexican males carry on like macho fools. The matador—a bullfighter in Mexico—makes the ultimate macho statement. He must stand alone, facing a furious animal that weighs up to 1,000 pounds (450 kg).

Though bullfighting capes are red or pink, bulls are actually color-blind. It is the movement of the cloth, not its color, that attracts their attention.

Bullfighting is wildly popular in Mexico. It was brought to Mexico from Spain. Some people denounce it as a bloody sport, a senseless display of cruelty to animals. Others hail it for its music, pageantry, and the courage and grace of the matador.

The bullring in Mexico City, the Plaza Mexico, is the largest such stadium in the world, seating fifty thousand people. Bullfights start at about 4:00 P.M. The spectacle begins with trumpet blasts, band music, and a colorful parade. Leading the parade are the three principal matadors. Usually each of the three matadors fights two bulls, one bull at a time. The matadors wear ornate costumes. Some bullfighters take up to two hours just to get dressed for a contest.

When the field is clear, the first bull is released from a pen. It rushes into the ring stomping, kicking, and full of fury. This is no barnyard bull. These animals are specially bred to fight. A novice bullfighter takes the first charges. The novice must stand motionless as the bull rips into his cape. Next comes a *picador*, who is mounted on a horse. The picador spears the bull with a long lance. Then three *banderilleros* rush up to the bull and stick sharply pointed poles into the back of its neck. At this point, the bull is wild with rage and pain. It is time for the matador to make his grand entrance.

The matador, showing no fear, approaches the animal while fluttering his cape. The bull charges again and again as the matador snatches the cape away. At each charge, the bull's pointed horns come perilously close to the matador's body. The crowd shouts *"Olé!"* when the matador makes a particularly daring or graceful move. By exhausting the animal with the repeated charges, the matador is controlling it, preparing the bull for the kill. Finally, the matador bends over the bull's bowed head with a sword in his hand. He thrusts the sword into the back of the bull's neck. The mighty bull is dead.

Is the bullfight cruelty or is it high drama? Is courage or brutal machismo on display in the bullfight? The debate may never be resolved.

A Love of Art

The Mexican Revolution of 1910 to 1920 left the country in shambles. Fields were barren, whole towns were abandoned, and nearly everyone had lost relatives in the fighting. Yet stars emerged from this destruction. The stars were not generals, politicians, or sports heroes. Instead, the idols of Mexican society were its artists.

The best of Mexico's artists were muralists. Murals are wall paintings, an ancient Mexican tradition. Hundreds of years ago, the walls of Mayan and Aztec temples were decorated with religious art. After the Mexican Revolution, three muralists—David Siqueiros, Diego Rivera, and José Orozco—won the admiration of the world. They are known today as the Big Three. Their murals and paintings are hailed as masterpieces.

David Siqueiros was as much a political activist as he was a painter. He was in and out of jail for his political activities. Siqueiros's murals were designed to uplift working men and women. "A muralist must have a theme," he once said. "His

Politics was the main subject of David Siqueiros's life and art. He became involved in the Mexican Revolution at age sixteen.

History According to Rivera

Diego Rivera's most famous mural is on the wall of the National Palace in Mexico City. The mural shows Rivera's interpretation of Mexican history. On the left side, he depicts native Mexicans living in peace and harmony. Then the Spaniards arrive and enslave them. On the right are scenes of Spanish brutality, including a Spaniard branding an indígena on the face with a hot iron.

mural is his pulpit." One of Siqueiros's murals shows poor farmers rising in revolution and seizing a flag from a landowner.

Many of Diego Rivera's murals also had a political slant. Rivera was the most popular of the Big Three among Mexicans. He stood 6 feet (1.8 m) tall, sported a scraggly beard, and weighed more than 300 pounds (140 kg). He once described himself as being "attractively ugly."

Rivera's wife, Frida Kahlo, was herself a celebrated artist. She painted pictures of her memories—the wonderful ones as well as the painful ones. Perhaps her most famous work is

Below left: **Diego Rivera and his wife, Frida Kahlo**

Below right: **Frida Kahlo painted** *The Two Fridas* **in 1939.**

The Two Fridas, a painting that shows two figures of her, side by side. One figure in the painting is loved, while the other is rejected by love. Kahlo suffered poor health most of her life. She also fought, sometimes furiously, with her more famous husband. Their battles made headlines in the Mexican press.

A less controversial painter was Rufino Tamayo. He worked primarily on canvas. Tamayo criticized the political nature of the Big Three muralists, claiming they were "engaged in journalism, not art." He learned to appreciate colors as a child from looking at his aunt's fruit stand. The brilliant yellows of the bananas and the rich greens of the limes surrounded the young Tamayo. It is no wonder that as a painter he became a master of color. Tamayo was in his nineties when he died in 1991. Factory workers, waitresses, and taxi drivers wept over his loss. The much-loved old man was the father figure of Mexican art.

Rufino Tamayo painted *The Grapefruit Seller* in 1958. Tamayo was known for his bold, bright style where everything looks bathed in sunlight.

Mariachi music can be happy or sad. One song may lament, *Mi vida no vale nada* ("My life is worth nothing"), while the next explodes with joyous words such as *Allá en el rancho grande, allá donde vivía* ("Out there on the great ranch where I used to live").

The Beat of Life

Think of Mexican music, and what comes to mind is the driving, toe-tapping beat of the mariachi band. Most mariachi bands are made up of one vocalist, two violinists, a guitar player, and two horn players. No rule governs this makeup. Throw in a bass violinist and subtract a horn player and you still have a mariachi band. The groups play in nightclubs and private parties, or they wander the streets playing for money. Their music throbs with life. The mariachi band is, like the cactus, a symbol of Mexico.

The Ballet Folklórico de Mexico was founded in 1952. The company presents dances that explore Mexican culture and history.

Mexicans also enjoy folk music, rock, jazz, classical music, opera, and ballet. Combining folk dancing with lively Latin music, the Ballet Folklórico de Mexico thrills audiences around the world. Members of the ballet wear brilliant costumes and dance with precision as well as passion. The Ballet Folklórico de Mexico serves as a great representative of the country.

Music is everywhere in Mexico. Bands play in restaurants, student groups sing in town squares, and guitarists sit on park benches and strum their tunes. Music is vital to the Mexican soul.

The Bellas Artes

In Mexico City, the Ballet Folklórico de Mexico performs in a theater building called the Bellas Artes. The theater was built about a hundred years ago. Constructed of heavy granite blocks, it cost the Mexican treasury millions of pesos. Today, it is slowing sinking. Mexico City is built on what was once a lake bed. The Bellas Artes is simply too heavy for the soft ground to support. Every year, the historic theater sinks a few more millimeters, and no one knows what can be done to stop it from eventually dropping out of sight.

Life in
Mexico

FOR CENTURIES, MEXICAN LIFE CENTERED ON THE RURAL village or small town. Farm people came to the village on Sundays to worship, shop, and visit friends and relatives. In rural towns, people lived a life that was unchanging, even timeless. Then, over the past forty years, farm people flocked to villages to live. Villages quickly became cities. Mexico now has about fifty cities of more than one hundred thousand people.

Rapid growth has altered life in towns and villages. Housing has popped up where cornfields and pastures once lay. Sadly, many of the outlying houses are little more than shacks. In Mexico, slums are generally found on the borders of towns, while rich people's houses stand in the center. Traffic jams in the old villages are now terrible. Pollution fogs the skies of mountain towns whose air was once pure.

Opposite: **A man takes part in a reenactment of the Battle of Puebla in 1862, in which Mexican troops defeated a much larger French force. The Cinco de Mayo holiday honors this victory.**

Many high quality goods are sold on the streets of Real de Catorce. A hundred years ago, fifteen thousand people lived in this mining town, but now it is home to only one thousand.

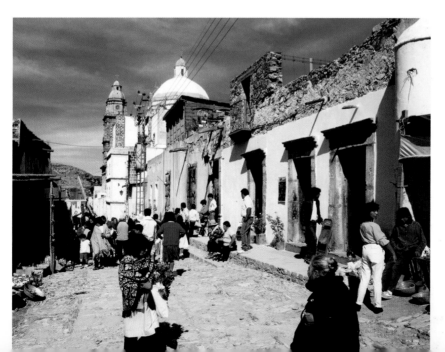

Life in Mexico **115**

Yet two elements resist change in Mexican village life: the town square remains the heart of a community, and the market is its social center. Most towns were laid out centuries ago in the Spanish style. Streets converge on the square at the center of town like spokes in a wheel. Typically, the square is a tree-shaded plaza. Villagers sit on benches in the tiny park or they walk slowly in the lanes. Squares are graced by statues and bubbling fountains. Mexicans are fiercely proud of their old plazas. They are kept spotlessly clean. The trees are not just trimmed—they are sculpted so that the treetops look like umbrellas.

Mexican towns are famous for their graceful, serene squares. These squares come to life in the evening as people gather to chat.

Cantinflas

The most popular star for generations of Mexican moviegoers was the comic Cantinflas (1911–1993). As a teenager, he had tried to become a boxer. His moves in the ring were so funny that the audience—and even his opponent—laughed. From boxing, Cantinflas graduated to films. His role was often that of a poor but honest workingman who survives on his ability to chuckle at his troubles. Movie critics have compared him to the silent screen star Charlie Chaplin. Chaplin saw one of Cantinflas's films and declared, "He's the greatest comedian alive!"

Invariably, a church rises at one end of the town square. Opposite the church might be a government building, which holds a courtroom, the office of the mayor, and perhaps a local jail. The plaza makes up the old downtown section. Nearby are hotels, a movie house, and the city's best restaurants. These days, the movie house may be little used since home video and cable TV have invaded Mexico. Video rental stores and noisy video-game parlors are now common. The town square springs to life at night. After work and after dinner, families come to the square to meet their neighbors and friends. Teenagers flirt. Tiny children dash up and down the lanes, playing tag or hide-and-seek.

Near the plaza is the village market. At its center is a squat building, holding dozens of stalls. Vendors—usually women— sell fruits and vegetables from these stalls. Market stalls also offer poultry, meat, clothes, and hardware items.

A woman spreads out her vegetables to sell at a market in Oaxaca.

So many vendors operate in the typical market that they spill out of the building and sell their goods outside. In some towns, the big building is called the closed market, while the outside section is called the open market. Outdoor vendors spread canvas on the sidewalks and sell pots and pans, CDs, or the latest style of tennis shoes. In many villages, Sunday is the traditional market day.

The market is more than a spot to buy and sell goods. It is an open-air meeting hall, a place to chat and gossip. Always colorful and always noisy, the market serves as village entertainment. Sellers shout out the prices of their goods, and buyers counter with the amount they are willing to pay. Friendly give-and-take haggling over prices is expected in a Mexican market. A customer who is not satisfied at one stand can simply move on to the next, because there are dozens to choose from.

As villages grow and modernize, the old markets face competition. Supermarkets, similar to those in the United States and Canada, have appeared on the fringes of towns. They are surrounded by parking lots. Inside, people push carts and take their groceries to checkout lines. No bargaining for prices

Taxco

Taxco is a famous traditional village in the state of Guerrero, high in the Sierra Madre Occidental. Scores of artists from the United States and Canada live there. Its Spanish colonial architecture is so charming that by law no changes can be made on the outside of its historic buildings. The village has a central plaza fronting a marvelous church. Taxco is known as the Silver City. It lies in the heart of what was once a silver-mining district. Today, dozens of talented silversmiths work and sell their crafts there.

here. Instead of the sounds of traditional haggling, shoppers hear the piped-in melodies of supermarket music. Prices are generally a few pennies cheaper at the modern places, but many people prefer the traditional market and its old ways. They remember years past when farm families would walk miles to come to town on a Sunday. A comfortable rhythm held sway when the market and the town square were the unrivaled highlights of village life. Many Mexicans still long for the old days.

Work and Leisure

The workday is also changing in Mexico. Not long ago, the vast majority of people either worked on farms or in small villages. Everyone worked close to home. Around noon, they came home to enjoy a large midday meal called the *comida*. After comida, while the sun was still high in the sky, families took a short nap, a *siesta*. Then people returned to their jobs and worked until about seven in the evening.

Modern industry now employs the bulk of Mexican workers. Factories demand that people stay at the workplace for eight to ten hours a day. The long comida followed by a siesta has been replaced by a half-hour lunchbreak. But Mexicans have not forgotten the simple pleasures of the midday comida. It is still enjoyed by millions of families on Sundays after church.

The Sunday comida is the time to invite guests. It is also the time for the cook—usually the mother—to display her skills. Perhaps she will prepare chicken covered with mole sauce. Mole is made of a dozen ingredients including

Tortillas are served at every Mexican meal. The color of the tortilla depends on the type of corn used to make it.

crushed nuts, chocolate, and spices. Some mole recipes are so treasured they are handed down in families as a sacred trust. The cook always serves a plate of steaming hot tortillas with the meal. Made of ground corn, the pancake-shaped tortilla is the everyday bread of Mexico. Everyone's favorite—tacos—are simply made with a filling such as cheese or meat rolled in a tortilla.

Enchiladas, often served for Sunday comida, are made by covering stuffed tortillas with a sauce and baking them. For a special Sunday dessert, the family enjoys flan, a rich pudding made from sugar and eggs.

A spicy hot chili sauce accompanies most Mexican meals. The hot sauce has led to the common belief that Mexican foods are fiery to the taste. Not true! Yes, the sauce is hot. It is made of chili peppers that are ground up with a little vinegar and water. A spoonful of chili sauce will set your mouth on fire. But this sauce is served as a side dish. That way, a diner can add as much—or as little—sauce as desired to the food. While many Mexicans enjoy chili sauce, others shun it.

After Sunday, the workweek begins anew. Workers go off to their jobs, and children return to school. Bringing education to all Mexicans has been a long and painful struggle.

Schools for All

During the Mexican Revolution, only 15 percent of the Mexican people could read and write. Few public schools existed at the time. Wealthy families sent their children to church-run schools that charged tuition. In the years after the revolution,

Mexican schoolboys sit in class at San Juan de las Manzanas. All Mexican children are supposed to attend school until age fourteen.

the government made an intense effort to build a modern public school system. But the system did not extend to the nation's distant rural areas. As a result, masses of farm children grew up without even seeing a textbook or the inside of a classroom. To this day, some Mexicans older than sixty cannot read or write because they never had the chance for an education.

The school system now extends to all children in every corner of Mexico. By law, children must attend school from ages six through fourteen. Students progress through three school levels. Primary school lasts from grades one through six. Next, the student enters secondary school for grades seven, eight, and nine. Preparatory school is a three-year program that can be compared to high school in the United States or Canada. After this, a student with excellent grades can apply to a university.

Mexico devotes more than 10 percent of its budget to education. Despite every effort, however, the system is plagued with dropouts. About half the students quit during secondary school. This means the children end their education before they reach age fourteen. Meanwhile, the Mexican economy becomes more

Street Schools

The Mexican government admits that at least two million children under age fifteen do not attend school. Many children who do not go to school are from poor families in the cities. As a result, many cities have established "street schools" where teachers educate kids in parks, vacant lots, or other classrooms without walls. In a corner of a busy downtown plaza in Guadalajara, about fifty kids sit on the concrete working on spelling lessons and math problems. Their "classroom" is marked off by chalk and white tape on the ground. It is hoped that these street schools will inspire the kids and their parents to get involved in the regular schools.

and more industrialized. The best-paying jobs are in computer science and other high-technology fields. No one who left school at fourteen is likely to qualify for a high-technology job.

Viva la Fiesta

It is a Saturday morning in June in the town of San Miguel de Allende in the state of Guanajuato. A woman walks down the sidewalk, lugging a shopping bag. Suddenly, a tall man snatches the bag away. He is wearing a black coat, like Count Dracula in the movies. The Dracula figure searches through the shopping bag. "What, no bottle of blood? You have no blood for me today?"

Is the woman alarmed? No. Instead she laughs, and so does Dracula. It is Loco Day in San Miguel. This costumed character is part of the advance party of the Loco Parade that is now winding down the street led by a brass band. *Loco* means "crazy." People in the parade look and act crazy. One "loco" wears the white cloak of a doctor and carries a saw as though he is ready and eager to operate on any bystander. A large woman is dressed like a female wrestler and challenges men to a match. No one accepts her offer. Loco Day is a time for everyone to go a little bit wild. In fact, that is the purpose of a Mexican fiesta—forget your cares and go nuts. After all, it's only for a day.

Any party, even a family get-together, is called a fiesta. Grand fiestas are celebrated by a town or by the nation. Family parties are joyful but limited to relatives and close friends. Grand fiestas know no such limits.

Masked figures parade through the streets of San Miguel de Allende on Loco Day.

Birthdays are acknowledged in Mexico, but a saint's day is greater cause for a family party. Most Mexicans are named after saints. Each saint has a feast day once a year. The feast day is also a day of celebration for anyone named after that saint. For example, if you are named after Saint Michael (your name would be Miguel if you are a boy, or Micaela if you are a girl), you celebrate the Feast of Saint Michael on September 29. A saint's day celebration has all the trappings of a typical birthday party in the United States. Guests bring gifts, candles are lit, and everyone eats cake and sings a special song.

Las Mañanitas

While the candles on the cake are burning, guests at a saint's day party sing "Las Mañanitas," a kind of "Happy Birthday" song. It has a haunting tune and poetic words:

Estas son las mañanitas	These are the little mornings
Que cantaba Rey David	That King David used to sing about
Y por el día de su santo	And for your saint's day
Que las cantamos aquí.	We are singing here.

Mexico's National Holidays

New Year's Day	January 1
Constitution Day	February 5
Flag Day	February 21
Birthday of Benito Juárez	March 21
International Workers' Day	May 1
Cinco de Mayo (Fifth of May)	May 5
Navy Day	June 1
Mexican Independence Day	September 16
Day of the Race	October 12
Revolution Day	November 20
Christmas	December 25

Local fiestas, those celebrated by a town, abound in Mexico. Veracruz is famous for its Carnival, the wild party given before Lent. In addition to Loco Day, San Miguel de Allende holds San Miguel (Saint Michael's) Day in late September. In theory, every Mexican named Miguel or Micaela is supposed to come to San Miguel to celebrate a collective Saint Michael's Day bash. Given the crowds and madness that take over the streets, it seems that all the millions of Miguels and Micaelas have indeed crowded into town.

Veracruz holds the largest Carnival celebration in Mexico. For nine days, both children and adults join in the parades and parties.

Two fiestas celebrated by the entire nation are Cinco de Mayo (Fifth of May) and Independence Day. Cinco de Mayo honors the 1862 Battle of Puebla in which a small Mexican force defeated an invading French army. Cinco de Mayo festivities include military parades, and politicians making patriotic speeches. Independence Day is a time for Mexicans to burst with patriotic pride. Independence is heralded with fireworks bursting in the night, bands playing the national anthem, and people shouting "Viva México! Viva México!"

Guadalupe Day combines patriotic pride with religious devotion. The Virgin of Guadalupe, the patron saint of Mexico, is the mother of all those who live in the land. She is the figure around which Mexicans join hands and truly call each other brothers and sisters. Under her banner, they proclaim with one voice: "Viva México! Viva México!"

Musicians and dancers perform in honor of the Virgin of Guadalupe. For many Mexicans, December 12, Guadalupe Day, is the most important holiday of the year.

Timeline

Mexican History

Corn is first cultivated in Mexico.	7000 B.C.
The Olmec civilization thrives on Mexico's Gulf Coast.	1250–400 B.C.
A mysterious people build the city of Teotihuacán near present-day Mexico City.	200 B.C.
Maya society reaches its peak.	A.D. 200–800
The Toltec civilization arises.	900
The Aztecs begin building Tenochtitlán (present-day Mexico City).	1325
The Spanish land in Mexico at present-day Veracruz.	1519
The Spaniards conquer the Aztecs and form New Spain.	1521
The Virgin of Guadalupe supposedly appears to Juan Diego.	1531
Father Hidalgo inspires the Mexican War of Independence.	1810

World History

2500 B.C.	Egyptians build the Pyramids and the Sphinx in Giza.
563 B.C.	The Buddha is born in India.
A.D. 313	The Roman emperor Constantine recognizes Christianity.
610	The Prophet Muhammad begins preaching a new religion called Islam.
1054	The Eastern (Orthodox) and Western (Roman) Churches break apart.
1066	William the Conqueror defeats the English in the Battle of Hastings.
1095	Pope Urban II proclaims the First Crusade.
1215	King John seals the Magna Carta.
1300s	The Renaissance begins in Italy.
1347	The Black Death sweeps through Europe.
1453	Ottoman Turks capture Constantinople, conquering the Byzantine Empire.
1492	Columbus arrives in North America.
1500s	The Reformation leads to the birth of Protestantism.
1776	The Declaration of Independence is signed.
1789	The French Revolution begins.

Mexican History

The War of Independence ends; Mexico becomes independent.	1821
Mexico cedes territory to the United States at the end of the Mexican-American War.	1848
The French army occupies Mexico.	1863–1867
Porfirio Díaz becomes president.	1876
The Mexican Revolution rages.	1910–1920
Lázaro Cárdenas becomes president and begins enacting economic reforms to help the poor.	1934
Hundreds of student protesters are massacred in Mexico City; Mexico becomes the first and only Latin American city to host the Olympics.	1968
Economic crises strike Mexico, and inflation goes out of control.	1970s
' A devastating earthquake strikes Mexico City.	1985
Mayan farmers calling themselves Zapatistas battle the Mexican army. The North American Free Trade Agreement (NAFTA) goes into effect.	1994
Vicente Fox Quesada becomes the first president in seventy-one years who is not a member of PRI.	2000

World History

1865	The American Civil War ends.
1914	World War I breaks out.
1917	The Bolshevik Revolution brings communism to Russia.
1929	Worldwide economic depression begins.
1939	World War II begins, following the German invasion of Poland.
1945	World War II ends.
1957	The Vietnam War starts.
1969	Humans land on the moon.
1975	The Vietnam War ends.
1979	Soviet Union invades Afghanistan.
1983	Drought and famine in Africa.
1989	The Berlin Wall is torn down, as communism crumbles in Eastern Europe.
1991	Soviet Union breaks into separate states.
1992	Bill Clinton is elected U.S. president.
2000	George W. Bush is elected U.S. president.
2001	Terrorists attack World Trade Towers, New York and the Pentagon, Washington, D.C.

Fast Facts

Official name: Estados Unidos Mexicanos (United Mexican States)

Capital: Mexico City

Official language: Spanish

Mexico City

Mexico's flag

The Yucatán Peninsula

National anthem: "Himno Nacional de México"
(National Anthem of Mexico)

Government: Federal republic

Chief of state and head of government: President

Area: 756,066 square miles (1,958,201 sq km)

Dimensions: East–west, 360 miles (579 km)
North–south, 976 miles (1,571 km)

Coordinates of geographic center: 23° 99' N, 102° 00' W

Bordering countries: To the north, the United States;
to the southeast, Guatemala and Belize

Highest elevation: Citlaltépetl (also called Orizaba), 18,410 feet
(5,610 m)

Lowest elevation: Mexicali Valley, 33 feet (10 m) below sea level

Average annual temperatures: Along the coast, 77°F (25°C);
in the mountains, 63°F (17°C)

Average annual rainfall: North-northwest, less than 10 inches (25 cm);
coastal plains, 40 to 115 inches (100 to 290 cm);
Chiapas highlands, more than 200 inches (500 cm)

National population (2004): 104,959,594

Taxco

Population of largest cities (2000):

Mexico City	8,591,309
Guadalajara	1,647,720
Ecatepec	1,620,303
Puebla	1,346,176
Netzahualcóyotl	1,224,924

Famous landmarks:
- ▶ *Bellas Artes*, Mexico City
- ▶ *Cañon del Rio Blanco National Park*, Veracruz
- ▶ *Chichén Itzá*, Yucatán
- ▶ *Copper Canyon*, south of Chihuahua
- ▶ *Metropolitan Cathedral*, Mexico City
- ▶ *Taxco*, Guerrero
- ▶ *Teotihuacán*, Mexico City

Industry: Mexican factories produce concrete, iron and steel, clothing, and electronics. Oil production is the second-largest contributor to the economy after manufacturing, while tourism is a major source of employment. Mining includes silver, copper, gold, lead, salt, and zinc.

Currency: The Mexican currency is the peso. In 2006, one U.S. dollar equaled 10.4 pesos.

Weights and measures: Metric system

Literacy: 86 percent

Currency

Schoolchildren

Frida Kahlo

Common words and phrases:		
	Bueno	Good
	¿Cómo está usted?	How are you?
	Gracias	Thank you
	Por favor	Please
	¿Qué hora es?	What time is it?

Famous Mexicans:		
	Carlos Chávez *Conductor and composer*	(1899–1978)
	Porfirio Díaz *Soldier and president*	(1830–1915)
	Vicente Fox Quesada *President*	(1942–)
	Miguel Hidalgo y Costilla *Priest and revolutionary*	(1753–1811)
	Benito Juárez *President*	(1806–1872)
	Frida Kahlo *Artist*	(1907–1954)
	José Clemente Orozco *Painter*	(1883–1949)
	Octavio Paz *Nobel Prize–winning writer*	(1914–1998)
	Diego Rivera *Painter*	(1886–1957)
	Rufino Tamayo *Artist*	(1899–1991)
	Francisco "Pancho" Villa *Revolutionary*	(ca. 1877–1923)
	Emiliano Zapata *Revolutionary*	(ca. 1879–1919)

To Find Out More

Nonfiction

▶ Bankston, John. *Diego Rivera.* Hockessin, DE: Mitchell Lane Publishers, 2004.

▶ Castillo, Ana. *My Daughter, My Love, the Eagle, the Dove.* New York: Dutton, 2000.

▶ Flowers, Charles. *Cortés and the Conquest of the Aztec Empire in World History.* Berkeley Heights, NJ: Enslow, 2001.

▶ Gritzner, Charles. *Mexico.* Philadelphia: Chelsea House, 2003.

▶ Reilly, Mary-Jo. *Mexico.* New York: Benchmark Books, 2002.

▶ Sanna, Ellyn. *Mexico: Facts and Figures.* Broomall, PA: Mason Crest Publishers, 2002.

▶ Steele, Christy. *Hispanic Culture.* Vero Beach, FL: Rourke Publishers, 2006.

▶ Stein, R. Conrad. *Pancho Villa: Mexican Revolutionary Hero.* Chanhassen, MN: Child's World, 2004.

Web Sites

▶ **The World Factbook: Mexico**
http://www.cia.gov/cia/publications/
factbook/geos/mx.html
*An excellent overview of the geography,
government, and economy of Mexico.*

▶ **The History Channel:
The History of Mexico**
http://www.historychannel.com/
exhibits/mexico/
*For a range of information about
Mexico's history, geography, people,
and culture.*

Organizations and Embassies

▶ **Embassy of Mexico**
1911 Pennsylvania Avenue, N.W.
Washington, DC 20006
202-728-1600

▶ **Mexican Government
Tourism Office**
405 Park Avenue, Suite 1401
New York, NY 10022
212-755-7261

Index

Page numbers in *italics* indicate illustrations.

Meet the Author

R. CONRAD STEIN was born and grew up in Chicago. He served in the U.S. Marines and later earned a degree in history from the University of Illinois. He then studied at and received an advanced degree from the University of Guanajuato in Mexico. Stein has published nearly two hundred books for young readers. He now lives in Chicago with his wife and their daughter, Janna.

Stein lived in Mexico through most of the 1970s. These years, he and his family spend each summer at their second home in the Mexican town of San Miguel de Allende. Over the years, Stein has seen vast changes in Mexico, but he still loves the country. At fiestas he proudly joins crowds on the streets and shouts out, "Viva México! Viva México!"

Photo Credits

Photographs © 2007:

Alamy Images: 121 (Rob Bartee), 29 bottom (Danita Delimont), 26, 28 (Sarkis Images), 35 (Janusz Wrobel)

AP/Wide World Photos: 106 (Guillermo Arias), 101 (Thomas Kienzle), 55 (Dario Lopez-Mills), 59 (Jose Luis Magana), 95 (Marco Ugarte), 47 (Rick Vasquez/Rumbo), 58, 81, 127 (Eduardo Verdugo)

Art Resource, NY: 111 (Museo de Arte Contemporaneo Internacional Rufino Tamayo, Reforma y Gandhi, Bosque de Chapultepec, Ciudad de Mexico), 110 right (Schalkwijk/© Banco de Mexico Trust, Museo Nacional de Arte Moderno, Mexico City, Mexico)

Bridgeman Art Library International Ltd., London/New York: 96 (Museo de America, Madrid, Spain/ Giraudon), 52 top (Museo Nacional de Historia, Mexico City, Mexico/ Giraudon)

Corbis Images: 49, 51, 53, 103, 108, 110 left, 133 bottom (Bettmann), 77 left, 122, 133 top (Keith Dannemiller), 40 (Leonard de Selva), 24 (Owen Franken), 48 top (Christel Gerstenberg), cover, 6, 113, 126 (Lindsay Hebberd), 117 (Hulton-Deutsch Collection), 89 (Janet Jarman), 70 (Kelly-Mooney Photography), 31 bottom (Kit Kittle), 16, 17, 23, 27, 65, 97, 98, 99 (Danny Lehman), 34 (Galen Rowell), 9 (Royalty-Free), 21 top (Nik Wheeler), 52 bottom

Danita Delimont Stock Photography/ David Sanger: 44

Getty Images: 112 (Stewart Cohen/ Taxi), 69 (Gabriel M. Covian/The Image Bank), 61 (Susana Gonzales/ Newsmakers), 64, 71 (Scott Olson), 105, 114 (Jorge Uzon/AFP)

Imagestate/Steve Vidler: 92

MapQuest.com, Inc.: 60, 131 top

Masterfile: 79 (Russell Monk), 100 (Rommel)

National Geographic Image Collection/ Maria Stenzel: 15

PhotoEdit/A. Ramey: 68

Robert Fried Photography: 2, 8, 10, 13, 14, 18, 36, 39, 42, 46, 56, 57, 62, 66, 73, 75, 76, 82, 91, 102, 118, 130 left, 131 bottom

South American Pictures/Tony Morrison: 29 top, 31 top, 45, 74, 87, 90

Superstock, Inc.: 21 bottom, 30, 33, 116 (age fotostock), 11 (Philip Beaurline), 22 (Angelo Cavalli), 7 bottom, 37, 119, 132 top (Yoshio Tomii), 67 bottom (Steve Vidler), 78, 132 bottom

The Image Works: 25 (Wesley Bocxe), 7 top, 83 (Bob Daemmrich), 32 (Sean Spague)

TRIP Photo Library: 88 (Martin Barlow), 80, 93, 125 (Esther James), 109 (Ken Mclaren), 115 (Colin Parker)

Viesti Associates, Inc.: 20 (Walter Bibikow), 104 (Ken Ross)

Maps by XNR Productions, Inc.